THE FALL OF BABYLON

THE FALL OF MAN'S SELF-RULE

This booklet is self published by Dr. Sharon Hanson, 25691 Co   Hwy 22, Erhard MN. 56534 Copyright © 2004 All rights reserved.

e-mail drsharon@prtel.com

Cover design by Victor Lundeen Company,

126-128 Lincoln Av. W.

Fergus Falls, Minnesota

ISBN 978-0-6151-5333-9

PREFACE

This book is the Gospel of the Kingdom which speaks of the building of the Great Mountain Kingdom of God in the earth through redemption and sanctification into spiritual maturity.

Amalek, the self-centered man will come to an end as the Lord defeats Amalek with the edge of His sword.

Exodus 17: 14 *"Then the Lord said to Moses, Write this for a memorial in the book and recount it in the hearing of Joshua, that I will utterly blot out the remembrance of Amalek from under heaven."*

The fire of God, during the restored Feast of Yom Kippur and the restored Feast of Tabernacles will bring about the Miracle of the Resurrection of the Gentile Son (Heathen Son). The time of harvest spoken of in Matthew 13:30 will be beginning.

This material contained in this book is heavy and needs to be carefully studied for it will bring His people into Life and the eternal kingdom. This material has been coming in revelation to me for over twenty years. I have purposely repeated many things in the better understanding for my reader. I have written it in the contents and then in summary have used the nine titles given me by the Holy Spirit to go over the material in greater simplicity.

The following nine titles were, *Amalek Our love of Self, Opening Daniel, Possessing our Promised Land, Restoring our Covenant with the King, and Temple of the Lord, and the Marriage of the (Bride) with the King, Building our House for the Lord, Heaven our Journey Home and The Sign of Jonah.*

Each of these titles has been written in the nine books with the same titles to give greater depth of understanding of each subject. The book *"Fiery Trials and Seducing Spirits" was given me later in time by the Holy Spirit, as I gained better understanding of what I had been through.*

The book the Fiery Trials and Seducing Spirits contains my personal testimony and would be helpful in your Battle for eternal righteousness.

The Revelation of the 1 Kings 17 passage reveals God's plan of redemption and harvest of the earth. He will revive the soul of the child of God and we will go from the age of rebellious Esau into the age of Obedient Jacob. Jacob held Esau's heel at birth. (Esdras, which is in the Apocrypha). This passage reveals there is no time interval between the two ages.

I see a victorious church however, I see a purified bride brought to total redemption by the work of the Holy Spirit.

I see an overcoming bride without spot or wrinkle washed in the blood of the Lamb.

In this passage of 1 Kings 17-23 Elijah means, "God of Jehovah," and is seen at the home of the widow (desolate place) of Zarephath (place of refinement). Her son had sickness, so there was no breath in him and Elijah prayed to the Lord for the child three times (three years pictured for the reviving of the bride of Christ). He prayed let this child's soul come back to him. Then the Lord heard the prayer of Elijah; and the soul of the child came back to him and he revived.

And Elijah took the child and brought him down from the upper room (Baptism of the Holy Spirit) into the house (of the Lord), and gave him to his mother, (Those that hear the word of the Lord and do it in Luke 21.)

And Elijah said, *"See your son (condition) lives."*

Many biblical scholars feel this child was Jonah (means, "Dove") and is the child of repentance from the pit of hell in the book of Jonah. A Dove is called, "O Perfect One" in The Song of Solomon.

This passage follows the passage of the drought in I Kings 17:1. Drought is defined as "Dry heat."

The drought is seen in Haggai, as the judgment that completes the temple in the Old Testament, which foreshadows the building of Christ's eternal temple in the days ahead.

The intense fire of seven times hotter than normal in their sin areas will bring God's people to repentance.

Sin will become very painful, which is revealed in Ezekiel 30:16.

Luke 12:49 *"I came to send fire on the earth, and how I wish it were already kindled."* Hebrews 12:29 reads, *"For our God is a consuming fire."*

TABLE OF CONTENTS

INTRODUCTION

The word Daniel means, "God is Judge." Daniel and the fall of Babylon (Iraq) are closely linked. The Lord is coming to judge the church and bring her into His barn of eternal righteousness. Matthew 13:30 *"First gather together the tares and bind them in bundles to burn them, but gather the wheat into my barn."*

We understand that the fall of man in the garden caused man's soul to merge or fall into our spirits. Thus, making the soul, the mind, will and emotions, rule man, rather than the spirit ruling the man.

This self-centered man is called Amalek in the scriptures. Amalek is Esau's grandson and follows the flesh, rather than following after his eternal inheritance of God.

In Exodus 17 God tells us He will fight Amalek from generation after generation, until the end when He will end the rule and remembrance of Amalek forever. I was told by the Holy Spirit "Man's self-rule is over."

Amalek is now being brought to an end through the dealings of God. Revelation 12 gives reference to the victory over the dragon and *"they loved not their lives unto the death*." In this spiritual death our soul is separated from our spirit and in God's Great Mountain Kingdom of righteousness man's spirit will rule his soul.

Our journey home is to surrender to the dealings of God that He might build us into new creations.

He takes us through the journey of the Israelites to possess the Promised Land of a freed soul.

We are brought to Gilgal, which is the place that the reproach of Egypt falls from us and this place is called the circumcision of the heart. In the Old Testament this was cutting away the flesh of the foreskin of the male, as a consecration to God. The circumcision of the heart is also a consecration to God.

We are to cross the Jordan in a decision to obey God and to be washed in the blood of the Lamb.

We are to deal with our Canaanite strongholds through repentance and we will be brought to restore our covenant with the God of the Universe at our personal Shechem. We are to cry to God for His righteousness with the surrender of our will to the will of the Lord, which will end our rebellion.

We open Daniel and see the child of God in a seventy year captivity, which Daniel saw. I also saw a 70 year Soviet Union Captivity of the Jews in the period from

1917-1987. This tells us along with the fall of the King of Babylon as Saddam Hussein, that we are in the time of the end of man's self-rule kingdom.

Jeremiah 25:12 *"Then it will come to pass, when seventy years are completed, that I will punish the king of Babylon and that nation, the land of the Chaldeans, for their iniquity, says the Lord; and I will make it a perpetual desolation."* This is modern Iraq in the natural realm, however, spiritual Babylon is our carnal nature and it will not rise again.

The book of Daniel reveals the image of the beast of self-rule kingdoms, as the world system. Daniel saw four beasts he called Babylon, Media-Persia and Greece and Rome.

In Daniel we see the king of Babylon or king of self-rule flesh that wanted all nations to bow down and worship this beast of self-pride, as an image of gold. Gold pictures what is precious to us.

If they did not bow down and worship this image they were thrown in the fire of refinement in God.

This refinement and what was to be accomplished in this fire can be illustrated by the 1 King's 17 account of the woman in Zarephath, which means, "refinement." This refinement was to restore the soul of the child of God and bring it to life. *"Believe to the saving of your soul."*

We see in Daniel 2:35 the Babylonian image ends with a STONE. The Bible interprets this large Stone as an altar before Jesus (Joshua) in 1 Samuel 6:14.

We know the Lion of Judah means, "An altar." We find in the Revelation of Jesus in Revelation 1:16 that He comes and out of His mouth went a two-edged sword. This is Jesus coming as the Living Word, bringing His people to repentance.

This stone altar where we lay our lives down in death to self is the stone that breaks our self-rule and ends the Babylonian image and our souls are separated by the sword of the Lord. Luke 2:35 *"Yes, a sword will pierce through your own soul also, that the thoughts of many hearts may be revealed."*

Daniel 2:35 reveals the stone breaks the image and brings us into the Great Mountain Kingdom of God.

Those born-again will not worship this image they will follow God and not the lusts of the flesh.

The fire seen in Daniel is our sins getting seven times hotter than normal and the intensity and pain of sin brings us to repentance.

    <u>Babylon our self-rule falls,</u> as we restore our Covenant of obedience to the Lord through the surrender of our will seen in Hebrews 10:9. The word of our testimony over the lies of the false prophet and our declared obedience to God through Deuteronomy 26:16 restores us to a covenant relationship.

The fall of Babylon is the fall of man's self-rule world system. It is the kingdom of the flesh. Babylon stands theologically for the community that is anti-God.

Babylon is defined as "The Gate of God." It is also interpreted as "Confusion."

The Lord has revealed Babylon to be a mystery and in Revelation 18 it is referred to as a harlot women. It is called a "Great City." Babylon is a Great City and Nineveh, Assyria is also referred to as a great city in the book of Jonah. The Great City Babylon is self-rule of our flesh and the Great City Nineveh is self-rule in our soul.

One of the earliest revelations I had with the Holy Spirit and this material was that the Old Testament Babylonians and the Old Testament Assyrians are a foreshadow of the New Testament flesh and the Devil.

Our victory over the flesh and the devil can be found illustrated by the victory of the Old Testament victory over the Babylonians and the Assyrians.

The world system was founded by Nimrod we see in Genesis 10 he started Babel and Nineveh. Nimrod was the giant son of Cush, Ham's son. Cush is known in Babylonian mythology as "The prophet of idolatry" and the "god of confusion." Ham is Noah's son and cursed of Noah.

Nimrod was the builder of Babylon known as Babel. This was the place of the tower of Babel and where God confused the nation's languages, because they were in one accord and nothing would be impossible for them. Nimrod built cities to be ruled by man, rather than the cities being ruled by God.

Nimrod and his image are seen in Daniel as Nebuchadnezzar, the King of Babylon, made people all over the world fall down and worship his image of the four part civilizations of mankind called Babylon, Media-Persia, Greece and Rome.

Babylon, as revealed by the Holy Spirit is the three part world system, the great cities of self-rule.

It is the political system of man. It is called the rule of the flesh. We then have the commercial system, as illustrating the lusts of the flesh. We then have a third part called Religious Babylon and that is the deception of the flesh. Man's traditions to get to heaven, rather than being born-again and Spirit filled.

The total surrender brings the total grace and mercy of God. He indwells His believers in the marriage of His bride, as He becomes one flesh with her.

  Our Temple is built by the command of Cyrus which is the pictured work of the Holy Spirit. It is built by the command of Darius, son of Cyrus. He was also known as Cambyses and in historical foreshadow we see the fire of Christ, as Cambyses destroyed all the temples not built for the God of Heaven in Egypt. Our temple is built by Artaxerxes, called the King of kings in Ezra 7:12. He is the restorer of the law into our temples.

We build Our House by confession, belief in the truth and the renewal of our minds, which happens due to the sword of the Lord and the Living Word, as our condition is brought to repentance on our own Mt. Moriah. This is called Salvation.

We possess our Promised Land of our soul by the surrender of our brother Esau and our fleshly desires. We vow to obey and are brought by the angel of the Lord to our own Mt. Carmel, where death to lies takes place in our soul, with our testimony for God over love of self and surrender of our will to God's will. When water of death is placed on our sins the fire comes from heaven and consumes our sin. This is called redemption.

When the fire of God brings forth great repentance we will see the miracle of the resurrected Gentile son, which will be the Sign of Jonah as the child of God is revived and brought to life in their souls. They will come to hear the word of God and do it. Then the glory of the Lord will cover the earth as the waters cover the sea.

The stone altar we place over the lions den of flesh will give victory over the stone tablets of the law and the victory over the stone law will deliver us from the stone covering our tombs.

Daniel 6:17 *"Then a stone was brought and laid on the mouth of the den."* The Stone Altar is mercy over judgment.

THE COMING FALL OF RELIGION

The house of Eli pictures the denominational priesthood. Now when Eli was 98 years old his eyes were dim and he could not see (religion will lose its vision and presence of God.) At this time Israel was fighting the Philistines, which means, "wallowing," and they decided to bring back the ark (obedience to the Ten Commandments) back unto themselves. They said when it comes among us it may save us from the hand of our enemies. The ark contains the law and the presence of God. Why some Christians now are having the manifest presence of the Lord in their meetings is that they are coming back into obedience to the laws of God through the power of the Holy Spirit.

But the Philistines heard about the ark coming back into the camp of the Israelites and they fought with Israel and captured the ark. When the ark was captured the two sons of Eli, Hohni and Phinehas died. Eli heard the news and fell off his chair and died.

Eli was the priest that had raised Samuel. It said, the word of the Lord was rare in those days and there was no widespread revelation. Eli's eyes had begun to grow dim so dim he could not see, and before the lamp went out in the tabernacle of the Lord, the Lord called out Samuel. Samuel heard the voice of the Lord and the Lord spoke to Samuel about the work that he was going to do against the house of Eli.

(1 Samuel 3:12-13-14) *"For I have told him that I will judge his house forever for the iniquity which he knows, because his sons have made themselves vile, and he did not restrain them.. And therefore I have sworn to the house of Eli that the iniquity of Eli's house shall not be atoned for by sacrifice or offering forever."*

The house of Eli's to be judged by God with no mercy, for they did not know the Lord and that the sons of Eli were corrupt and did not restrain their sons from evil.

The true church of Samuel, the called out ones went out to defeat the Philistines and will have victory over the temples of the Philistines, as Samson pulled down their lying temples.

The defeat of lies is to bring the ark of truth back into our temples and the truth will bring the defeat of the Philistines (sickness etc.).

Saul is another picture of the house of religion that persecuted the real believer David. Saul died in the battle with the Philistines. A spear went through him as he leaned on his spear, but an Amalekite in 2 Samuel 1:8 finally killed him. He had let the Amalekite live in 1 Samuel 15:9, in disobedience to God.

Satan's religion has always one clearly defined mark in the omission of the gospel of Calvary, which is the atoning death of the Son of God and His propitiation for sin. His blotting out sin for us and crucial His not telling the people of their deliverance from the power of sin and the flesh by the severing power of the cross. Nor, do they tell the people of His call of the blood redeemed soul to the cross in death to self and sacrifice for others.

The church today is very Laodicean, neither hot nor cold in America, as they often are seeker sensitive in other words we worship God, but we don't want God to show up to offend our friends. The Holy Spirit and His gifts and manifestations might offend some. How that must offend the heart of God. Matthew 11:6 *"**Blessed is he who is not offended because of Me.**"*

The Holy Spirit spoke to me and said, *"I want to touch My people, refresh My people, but the churches won't let me in."*

BABYLON, THE HEAD OF THE IMAGE

The old Babylonian civilization is in the area of Iraq, on the banks of the Euphrates in the land of Shinar. (Wickedness is to return in the visions of Zechariah).

Babylon was at its height of power in 2000 B.C.

Genesis ascribes the foundation of the city to Nimrod. The next or middle Babylonian period was the recovering of Marduk's statue. He was the head god in the Babylonians pantheon of gods. During the Assyrian supremacy Sennacherib removed the stature of Marduk. The removal of Saddam Hussein's stature as the King of Babylon reveals where we are, as we may be headed for the Chaldean rulers as God's judgment people of Habakkuk.

The Chaldeans are the last period of Babylon in the Old Testament and I believe in the end of the age.

The old city of Babylon was built by Nebuchadnezzar with its hanging gardens and wide city walls. Hilah is the old city of Babylon today. Saddam rebuilt a great deal of the old city.

Babylon is the head of the image in the account of the four beasts of world civilizations Media Persia, Greece and Rome in the book of Daniel. It is the head of gold and its animal is the lion.

Nebuchadnezzar built an image and wanted everyone to bow down to it and worship it. (This is the image of the beast and believers must not worship things in the world system, rather than total worship of God.)

Saddam Hussein claimed to be the revived Nebuchadnezzar, as he rebuilt a great deal of Old Babylon.

When we open the book of Daniel which means, "God is judge" we find the children of Israel in captivity to Babylon (self-rule intense).

We find that Daniel's friends are thrown into a fiery furnace and because they trusted in their God and frustrated the King's word (believed God's word over the World's) and would not worship any other god, but their own God they were thrown into the fiery furnace. But the angel of the Lord was in the furnace with them and they were delivered even though the heat was turned up seven times hotter than normal.

It states in Revelation 18:23 that by Babylon's sorcery all the nations were deceived, for she is called the great harlot.

In Daniel 7:4 we see the first beast was Babylon and it was like a lion, and had Eagles wings. It was lifted up from the earth and made to stand on two feet like a man and a man's heart was given to it. It became an image of the rule of man.

Malachi 3:3 *"He will sit as a refiner and a purifier of silver that they may offer to the Lord an offering in righteousness."*

Micah 4:10 *"And you shall even go to Babylon. There you shall be delivered; there the Lord will redeem you from the hand of your enemies."*

CHAPTER ONE

THE ISRAEL FEASTS RESTORED IN

THE EARTH

YOM KIPPUR

In the material I have received from the Holy Spirit I have seen with spiritual eyes the coming of the Lion of Judah to bring His people to repentance. The Lion of Judah means, "Altar." I then received insight that this is a Yom Kippur or a coming Day of Atonement.

In the book *"The Feasts of Israel"* by Bruce Scott the following paragraphs opened my eyes to the restoration of the feast of Yom Kippur in the earth with the coming fire of God.

"Yom Kippur was to provide an atonement (covering) for sin, for the Holy of Holies in the tabernacle, for the tabernacle itself, for the altar of incense in the Holy Place, for priests (including the High Priest), and for the sins committed in ignorance by the people of Israel."

"Yom Kippur was divinely ordained because of uncleanness of the children of Israel, and because of their transgressions in all their sins."

Bruce Scott sees the passage in Deuteronomy 30:1-6 of Israel's repentance, Israel's regathering, and Israel's revival.

Deuteronomy 30 1-6 "Now it shall come to pass, when all these things come upon you, the blessing and the curse which I have set before you, and you call them to mind among the nations where the Lord your God drives you, and you return to the Lord your God and obey His voice, according to all that I command you today, you and your children, with all your heart and with all your soul, that the Lord your God will bring you back from captivity, and have compassion on you and gather you again from all the nations where the Lord your God has scattered you.

"If any of you are driven out to the farthest parts under heaven, from there the Lord your God will gather you, and from there He will bring you. Then the Lord your God will bring you into the land which your father's possessed, and you shall possess it. He will prosper you and multiply you more than your fathers.

"And the Lord your God will circumcise your heart and the heart of your descendants, to love the Lord your God with all your heart and with all your soul, that you may live."

This passage goes on to explain that they will again obey the voice of the Lord and obey all His commandments. This happens as they receive the gift of the Father of a new heart and a new Spirit.

A Jew is one that is circumcised inwardly in the heart Romans 2:28-29. Israel the natural and Israel the spiritual bride are all moving in exact parallel. Israel the natural is the pattern for Israel the spiritual. 1 Corinthians 15:46 *"However, the spiritual is not first, but the natural, and afterward the spiritual."*

Yom Kippur the great Day of Atonement, will be restored in the entire earth, as the spring feasts like Passover and Pentecost have been restored.

THE FEAST OF TABERNACLES

The Feast of Tabernacles is another fall feast of Israel which will also be restored in the earth with the resulting fire offerings (sin offerings for the fire of God to consume our sins). Peace offerings that will bring us peace in our soul and the burnt offerings of total surrender.

The Feast of Tabernacles is the feast of ingathering and pictures the days of Messiah.   Leviticus 23:33 " *These are the feasts of the Lord which you shall proclaim to be holy convocations, to offer an offering made by fire to the Lord, a burnt offering and a grain offering, a sacrifice and drink offering, everything on its day."*

Pop and coffee, white bread and sugar gave me peace and healed my migraine headaches. These offerings were for my benefit. The fire offering was the sin of lust that definitely gave me peace. The fire of judgment came against this and sin became very painful to bring me to repentance.

Jesus is our sacrifice for sins and because of this great gift of redemption we can have our sins consumed in the Fire of the Holy Spirit.

Our God is a consuming fire in Hebrews 12:29 and when we have our Mt. Carmel experience with God we put the water of death on the sins and the fire from heaven comes down and will consume our sins. Thus, Mt Carmel is a picture of redemption, which is the removal of sins.

Mt. Moriah is surrender to God, and pictures salvation, as Abraham surrendered his only son and the ram became his substitute. Son can be defined as a "condition." <u>Mt **Moriah is salvation**</u>, which means the process of being saved.

But our <u>**Mt. Carmel experience is redemption,**</u> which is a choice we make before God to choose to worship God over the love of our self nature and our sins. A place we die to self and cross over the Jordan River to be washed in the Blood of the Lamb.

Redemption is the sins being removed by the consuming fire of God and we come into Christ's righteousness, because we need to cry out to obey the law, which we cannot do on our own.

The Feast of Tabernacles is a seven day feast which will be duplicated in the seven years of Jacob's Trouble. Jeremiah 30:7.

Jacob is obedient Israel who followed his birthright of eternity. Jacob is delivered out of the trouble because he obeys the Lord and gets redeemed. Jacob therefore pictures all obedient believers not just the Jewish nation in Israel. Jacob follows the Spirit not the flesh as Esau did.

The Feast of Tabernacles is the feast that sees the days of Messiah. It predicts the restored house of David. David is the king of all Israel. Spiritually he is free. The scripture in 2 Samuel 3:21 reveals he is king over all his hearts desires. And in 1 King 14:8 David followed God with all his heart. "*David did all My will*," said the Lord in Acts 13:22.

THE NEW COVENANT IS A SURRENDERED WILL

In Hebrews 10:9 we see the restored new covenant where the law will be written on our heart. "Then he said,

"Behold I have come to do your will, 'O God." "He takes away the first that He may establish the second."

Jesus taught us how to go through the cross when He said, *"Not what I will, but what You will"* in Mark 14:36.

The Feast of Tabernacles predicts the time of the Messianic age will be the time of the Shekinah glory, as the presence of God dwells with Israel (Natural and spiritual).

He will have taken His people into the holy of holies, through the veil and into obedience to the Ark of the Covenant. Christ brings the bride into His righteousness, for He comes to fulfill the law not abolish it, Matthew 5:17.

1 Corinthians 15:54 ***"So when this corruptible has put on incorruption, and this mortal has put on immortality, then shall be brought to pass the saying that is written: "Death is swallowed up in victory."***

Going through the veil is passing from death unto life and 2 Corinthians 3:16 reads, *"Nevertheless when one turns to the Lord, the veil is taken away."*

Bruce Scott also states that the seventh day of the festival is known as "Hoshana Raba" or the "**Great Hosanna**." The world will rejoice and observe the Feast of Tabernacles, during the earthly reign of the Messiah.

CHAPTER TWO

THE COMING FIRE OF THE LION

OF THE TRIBE OF JUDAH

The words "the Lion of the Tribe of Judah" means, "Altar." The word Judah means, "Praise." The fire of the Lion of Judah will bring the people of praise to the altar before Him. The Pillar of fire which is the intensity of sin areas will lead the bride to repentance and the cloud of His presence will guide them to safety.

Luke 12:49 "*I came to send fire on the earth, and how I wish it were already kindled*!" Part of that fire is also standing against the persecution of family and friends for the cost of the discipleship of Christ

WASH OUR CLOTHES AND BE READY FOR THE THIRD DAY

Exodus 19:10-11 "*Then the Lord said to Moses, "Go to the people and sanctify them today and tomorrow, and let them wash their clothes, and let them be ready for the third day. "For on the third day the Lord will come down upon Mt. Sinai in the sight of all the people."*

Mt. Sinai is a reference to the law that was given as the Ten Commandments. The Lord will come down on obedience to the Ten Commandments. He will bump His people right up against obedience to the law and this will require a choice of obeying God or following the flesh and their sensual desires.

What is meant by the third day? The third day is three thousand years for Hosea reveals a day is like a thousand to the Lord. In the year 2001 A.D, I received a song from the Lord that a prophet had spoken to me about earlier. This song said, *"It is a new day in the Camp of the Lord, Get your lamp filled with the glory of My son."*

We have entered the third day and we must now wash our clothes in the blood of the Lamb.

What do we mean by washing our clothes? Genesis 35:2 *"And Jacob said to his household and to all that were with him, "Put away the foreign gods that are among you, purify yourselves, and change your garments."*

WASH OUR CLOTHES WITH FIRE AND WATER

Water is a picture of death many times in scripture, as in the days of Noah water of the flood caused the death of the wicked. Water in Baptism pictures death of our sinful nature and is an outward sign of the inward work of the cross.

In the story of Elijah in the book of Kings we see Elijah put water on the sacrifice and then called on heaven to burn up the sacrifice and fire came down from heaven and burned up the sacrifice. Put the water of death on our sacrifice, *"Help, Lord I do not want to do this anymore."* Repentance is total turning from our sin. The Lord said in Isaiah 59 *"I will redeem those in Zion who turn from their transgressions."*

Numbers 31:24 "And you shall wash your clothes on the seventh day (the seventh thousandth years from Adam (same as the third day from Christ) and be clean and afterward you may come into the camp (kingdom). 2001 A.D. was approximately moving us into the seventh day.

Numbers 31:23 "Everything that can endure fire, you shall put through the fire, and it shall be clean, and it shall be purified with the water of purification, but all that cannot endure fire you should put through water (die to it).

Romans 7:6 "We die to the things that hold us."

THE ANGEL OF THE LORD IN THE FIRE WITH THEM

Daniel 3:6 reveals those that are cast into the fire of refinement are those that do not bow down and worship the image that Nebuchadnezzar had set up. We have discussed that this is the image of the world system, which is designed to show us the desires of our heart.

"And whoever does not fall down and worship shall be cast immediately into the midst of a burning fiery furnace.

31

When all the people heard the sound of music all the people, nations, and languages fell down and worshipped the image, which King Nebuchadnezzar had set up."

Daniel's friends are cast into the burning fiery furnace and they were told, *"Who is the god that will deliver you from my hands?" Daniel 3:17 "If that be the case, our God whom we serve is able to deliver us from the burning fiery furnace, and He will deliver us from your hand, O king."*

The fire had no power over the bodies of Daniel's friends for their God sent an angel and delivered His servants who trusted in Him, and they have frustrated the kings word, and yielded not their bodies, that they should not serve nor worship any god except their own God."

Exodus 23:20-23 "Behold, I send an angel before you to keep you in the way and to bring you into the place which I have prepared. Beware of Him and obey His voice; do not provoke Him, for He will not pardon your transgressions; for My name is in Him.

"But if you indeed obey His voice and do all that I speak, then I will be an enemy to your enemies and an adversary to your adversaries."

"For My angel will go before you and bring you in to the Amorites and the Hittites and the Perizzites and the

32

Canaanites and the Hivites and the Jebusites; and I will cut them off."

THE FIRE IS TO BRING FORTH THE MIRACLE OF THE RESURRECTION OF THE GENTILE SON.

The fire will restore the souls of the children of God. The passage in Hebrews 10:39 *"But we are not of those who draw back to perdition, but of those who believe to the saving of the soul (mind, will, and emotions)."*

The souls will be restored and brought to life eternal and brought back to hearing and doing the will of God.

THE FIERY TRIAL 1 PETER 4:12

"Beloved, do not think it strange concerning the fiery trial which is to try you, as though some strange thing happened to you; but rejoice to the extent that you partake of Christ's sufferings, that when His glory is revealed, you may also be glad with exceeding joy."

In identifying the factors involved in **the fiery trial** we look to the two kings that were defeated by Moses as the children of Israel began to enter the Promised Land on the East of the Jordan. Before they crossed the Jordan in self-death they had to defeat these two kings that picture for us passion and lust.

Og king of Bashan and his territory, who was of the remnant of the giants, who dwelt at Ashtoreth and at Edrei in Joshua 12:4, 2. Then there was Sihon king of the Amorites, who dwelt in Hesbon and ruled half of Gilead..." Ashtoreth is the fertility goddess of the Philistines and Gilead means, *"To have affection for sexually or otherwise."* Giants are sins and these sins are defeated as we go to God for His righteousness. We must obey the law and we need the grace of the Lord in His marriage at Cana, the place of grace and mercy.

Agag is the king of the Amalekites and the word means, **"Fiery flame**." Haman in the book of Esther is an Agagite or Amalekite. Amalek is the grandson of Esau and is the love of self or the self-centered man. Haman's defeat reveals the providential circumstances that defeat the flesh as it tries to destroy the Jews, the people of God. Amalek pictures the pride of man and comes as the Grecian beast of Revelation 17 with the ten kings. This beast is worldly wisdom and self-serving other gods. Haman and his ten sons were hanged on the gallows, rather than the Jews.

The Lord will finally blot Amalek out from under heaven we read in Exodus 17.

The Lord said He would have war with Amalek from generation to generation in Exodus 17, but in the end He would utterly blot out the remembrance of Amalek from under heaven and we have arrived at that time in history.

We are at this point in time when not only Exodus 17 will be fulfilled, but also Daniel 9, which reveals in the seventieth week sin and transgressions, will end.

That can only happen through the work of the Holy Spirit in the souls of His people.

This fiery trial also is called the **fiery red dragon** in Revelation 12. This means it is a sin dragon. Our sins are as scarlet. To identity the dragon we see it is the devil and the serpent of old. The serpent of old deceived Eve to disobey God. Under the testing of this dragon we will be called to choose God over this **fiery serpent** of deceit and reverse the curse of the fall.

The dragon planet is Venus as it had **fiery tails** hanging from it in days of old. Venus is the planet worshipped as the bull and was the Apis Cult of the golden calf at the bottom of Mt. Sinai.

Daniel 7:9 *"And the ancient of Days was seated; His garment was white as snow, and the hair of His head was like pure wool. His **throne was a fiery flame**, Its wheels a burning fire; **A fiery stream** issued and came forth from before Him."*

*Hebrews 10:26 "But a certain fearful expectation of judgment, and **fiery indignation** which will devour the adversaries."*

FIRE TO END EDOM (flesh-rule)

Jacob and Esau were twins and two nations were to be separated from Rebekah's womb.

Jacob followed after his eternal birthright while Esau followed the lust of the flesh.

Jacob held Esau's heel at birth and a passage in Esradas in the Apocrypha reveals there will be no interval between the ages of rebellious Esau and obedient Jacob.

Obadiah is the book of the Bible that deals with the fall of Edom and the house of Esau.

In Obadiah 1:1, 15-17 *"Thus says the Lord God concerning Edom (we have heard a report from the Lord, and a messenger has been sent among the nations, saying, "Arise, and let us rise up against her for battle.")* In 2001 we heard the report to fight against the evil nations from President Bush, as he fulfilled Obadiah 1:1.

"For the day of the Lord upon all nations is near; as you have done, it shall be done to you; your reprisal shall return upon your own head."

"But on Mount Zion there shall be deliverance, and there shall be holiness; The house of Jacob shall possess their possessions, the house of Jacob shall be a fire, and the house of Joseph a flame; but the house of Esau shall be

stubble; They shall kindle them and devour them, and no survivor shall remain of the house of Esau," "For the Lord has spoken."

Jacob fled from brother, Esau (carnal flesh) in Genesis 35:1. Jacob went toward Haran (to end the temple of sin which is located in Haran.) He stopped near Bethel, which was the old Hittite city of Luz. This statement helps us identify the Hittites as the lust of the flesh, for Jacob turned from brother, Esau.

He made a vow before God to obey God if God would take care of him. It said he laid his head on a stone (altar).

Following his vow before God Jacob had a dream vision of a ladder where angels were ascending and descending. Jacob named Bethel the "Gate of heaven."

In Exodus 23:20 we read that God sends an angel of the Lord, to bring His people into the place He has prepared for them, which is the place of abiding rest for their souls.

Micah 7:9 *"He will bring me forth to the light, and I will see His righteousness."*

We find that the prayer of Jacob brought the angel and our vow of obedience also brings the angel, to bring us into the eternal kingdom.

In the book of Daniel we see that the angel Gabriel came when he prayed, speaking and confessing his sin and the sin of his people and presenting his supplication before the Lord for the Holy Mountain (righteousness of God).

THE FIRE OF GOD TO BRING ABOUT THE SEPARATION OF THE NATIONS

Matthew 13:30 *"Let both grow together until the harvest, and at that time of harvest I will say to the reapers, "First gather together the tares and bind them in bundles to burn them, but gather the wheat into My barn."*

Matthew 13:38, 39 *"The field is the world, the good seeds are the sons of the kingdom, but the tares are sons of the wicked one." "The enemy who sowed them is the devil. The harvest is at the end of the age, and the reapers are the angels."*

Matthew 13:49 *"So it will be at the end of the age. The angels will come forth, separate the wicked from among the just, and cast them into the furnace of fire."*

GENESIS DEFINATIONS REVEAL THE COMING SEPARATION

Abraham (father of many nations marries (dwells with Sarah (Hidden Queen).

Sarah gives birth to the child of promise, the child of the free women called Isaac, which means, "Laughter."

Isaac (the child of promise) marries (dwells with) Rebecca, which means, "Fettering by beauty" and that means to us "lust."

Isaac and Rebecca give birth to twin sons called twin nations in Genesis 25:23. In these two sons the Lord had said *"that there were two nations in your womb, two peoples shall be separated from your body."*

In these two nations we see the separation of the righteous from the wicked or carnal fleshly sons. (Sodom and Gomorrah was a carnal city, and a burnt city in Genesis 19:5.)

1. Jacob means, "To supplant, restrain, to clog or circumvent." Jacob restrains or circumvents lust through Christ. He wrestles with God and becomes spiritual Israel at Peniel by Bethel (the gate of heaven). Genesis 35 he turned from his brother Esau (rebellious flesh).

Jacob marries Rachel which means, "Sheep" <u>Jacob dwells as a sheep</u>.

2. Esau means, "To do or commit, felt." Esau dwelled with or married Canaanite women. He committed lust and did not deal with it through God. His grandson was called Amalek, which pictures our love of self. He gave up his eternal birthright for a fleshly appetite. Esau founded the

nation of Edom and Amalek founded the Amalekites and they were the nation that would not let Israel cross into their land to go into Canaan. The Israelites had to go all the way around to the Jordan to enter the Promised Land. This shows us we must go through the blood of the Lamb in death to self in order to have victory over our love of self. He gave up his eternal birthright for a fleshly appetite. Esau founded the nation of Edom. The word means, "red" and red means, "sin."

Lot means, veil and the veil was removed from Sodom and Gomorrah in Genesis 19:5 and Lot is rescued by Abraham, but the veil gave birth to illegitimate sons (daughters gave birth to Moab and Ammon.) This tells us that if we don't go through the veil and pass from death unto life we will be illegitimate sons of God.

Christ made a new and living way for us to pass through the veil that is His flesh, with the surrender of our will to the will of the Lord Hebrews 10:9.

In the testing of the false prophet, who desolates our temple mount with a sin –idol, to get us to worship the world image, as the image of the beast, the nations will be separated as to those that worship the flesh and those that follow the Lord.

Multitudes of No are to be cut off in Ezekiel 30:15.

"I will pour My fury on Sin, the strength of Egypt; I will cut off the multitude of No, and set fire in Egypt; Sin shall have great pain."

CHAPTER THREE

THE FALL OF BABYLON THROUGH

THE FIRE OF THE LIVING WORD

The fall of Babylon from our soul happens through the living word as the Living word separates our soul from our spirit and Babylon self-rule falls to the rule of God.

Confusion falls to the truth of God's Word. Flesh desires fall to the desires of God with the surrender of our will to the will of the Father.

THE SWORD

Isaiah 34:5 "*For My sword shall be bathed in heaven; indeed it shall come down on Edom, and on the people of My curse for judgment.*"

The word of God is the sword of the Lord and it discerns the thoughts and desires of our heart.

Hebrews 4:12 "*For the word of God is sharper than any two –edged sword, piercing even to the division of soul and spirit, and joints and marrow, and is a discerner of the thoughts and intents of the heart.*"

The commander of the Lord appears with a sword drawn in His hand in Joshua 5:13. This sword appeared when

Joshua was by Jericho at the entrance to the Promised Land. This passage follows the passage of the circumcision, as they were now ready to take the territory of the enemy of their Promised Land (souls). In Isaiah 61 the conquering king is taking vengeance on his enemies.

In the fall of man in the garden man fell into himself and his soul ruled his spirit. The Lord through the Living Word, is going to restore us from the fall and come as we see in Revelation 1:16. *"Out of His mouth went a sharp two-edged sword and His countenance was like the sun shining in its strength."*

This division of our soul from our spirit is called the circumcision of our heart. It becomes, as did the circumcision of the flesh in the Old Testament, a consecration to God.

It is the end of Babylon self-rule, self-will and self-love. We come out of the Babylonian kingdom and through a stone altar before Jesus (Joshua in 1 Samuel 7:14.) we will fulfill Collisions 2:13-14.

"He has delivered us from darkness and translated us into the kingdom of the Son of His love." "In whom we have redemption through His blood, the forgiveness of sins."

We see in Genesis 3:6 the fall involved the lust of the flesh, the lust of the eyes, and the pride of life.

In 1 John 2:16 *"For all that is in the world, the lust of the flesh, the lust of the eyes, and the pride of life is not of the Father, but is of the world."*

In the book of Daniel, which means "God is judge" we find God's people are held captive in Babylon.

Daniel read Jeremiah's prophecy that after seventy years in Babylon God would punish the King of Babylon. So he started making intercession for God's people to come out of Babylon.

In our day we have seen the Jews in captivity in the Soviet Union for seventy years from 1917 to 1987. We have recently seen the punishment and death of the King of Babylon Saddam Hussein and the deliverance of 50,000 people of Iraq.

Thus President Bush fulfilled again the exact acts of Cyrus king of Persia, in the Old Testament fore-shadow of the fall of Babylon.

WHY DOES IT FALL?

The handwriting on the wall in Daniel gave us three words supernaturally written on the wall of the temple of Babylon, Mene, Mene (means "mind") and the days of man ruling himself are numbered!

The word Tekel calls Babylon self-rule a deficient kingdom.

Parsin or Upharsin-Babylon falls to the Medes and the Persians, which reads, *"those that are intent on conquering."*

Cyrus, a picture of the work of the Holy Spirit, is king of our divided self of Persia, but the Medes contained Nineveh in their land. Nineveh was a place of rebellion from God. Persia means, "Divided." When we conquer our Nineveh carnal nature, we are made whole and come into the eternal kingdom of God.

Genesis 4:7 *"If you do well, will you not be accepted? And if you do not do well, sin lies at the door. And its desire is for you, but you should rule over it."*

BABYLON FALLS AT REGENERATION

Regeneration means, receiving a whole new nature from heaven, as we are born-again from heaven. Where we meet God at the mercy seat and receive His righteousness.

Revelation 18:14 *"And the fruit that your soul longed for has gone from you, and all the things that are rich and splendid have gone from you and you shall find them no more."*

FALLEN ADAM IS 666 OR UNREGENERATED MANKIND.

The Revelation 13 scripture states the number of the beast is the number of a man. It is the same passage as the "Beast out of the Earth" or the false prophet that brings about our regeneration, as we choose God over the serpent of deceit.

Two Babylon's by Alexander Hislop gives us this description in ancient Chaldee and Greek. *"Janus was properly Eanus, and in ancient Chaldee Eanus which signifys "The Man."*

In Greek it becomes Osiris, the name Eanush, or as it appeared in the Egyptian language, Phanesh, "The Man was only the name of our great progenitor. The man Adam in Hebrew of Genesis almost always occurs with the article before it implying "The Adam or The Man." There is a difference however, "The Adam" refers to the man unfallen Eaush," "The Man," to fallen man.

" The fountain and the father of the gods," is fallen Adam the principal of pagan idolatry went to exalt fallen humanity, to consecrate its lusts, to give men license to live after the flesh, and yet, after such a life, to make them sure of eternal felicity. Eanus the fallen man was set up as the human head of this system of corruption this is the "Mystery of Iniquity."

June Lewis in her book *From Dust to Glory* reveals that the New Testament book of Romans is the sixth book and the sixth chapter and the sixth verse. This is the circumcision verse. *"Knowing this that our old man was crucified with Him, that the body of sin might be done away with, that we should no longer be slaves to sin." 666 refers to fallen unregenerated mankind that is not born-again.*

Revelation 13:8 *"And all who dwell on the earth will worship him, whose names have not been written in the Book of Life of the Lamb slain from the foundation of the world."*

THE KINGDOM OF BABYLON, THE GREAT CITY OF HARLOTRY OF SELF-RULE AS THE IMAGE OF THE BEAST.

The purpose of the image is to reveal to us the thoughts of our heart in Daniel 2:30.

The book of Daniel reveals this image as the nations of four civilizations in which self-rule rides on the back of this scarlet beast. However, the book of Revelation sees all seven mountain civilizations carrying the scarlet beast of self-rule. I have a picture of Europa riding on the back of Zeus. Europa is one of the moons of Jupiter. (Jupiter is also Zeus). Could this refer to Europe?

Daniel 2:34,35 *"You watched while a stone was cut out without hands, which struck the image on its feet of iron and clay (time of the Roman iron will coming against the clay of the believer,) and broke them in pieces."*

*"And the **<u>stone that struck the image</u>** became a great mountain and filled the whole earth."*

The Christ coming as the Lion of the Tribe of Judah, brings the believer to the Stone altar and delivers His people out of bondage to self-rule.

The Stone is identified in 1 Samuel 6:14 *"Then the cart came into the field of Joshua of Beth Shemesh, and stood there; a large stone was there. So they split the wood of the cart and offered the cows as a burnt offering to the Lord."*

Daniel himself was thrown into the Lion's Den (flesh rule), which pictures our flesh. A stone was put over the mouth of the den. He prayed and the lions did not hurt him.

We as the body of Christ are commanded to come out of Babylon. We are to come out of the love of the things of the world, lest we share in her sins, and lest you receive of her plagues in Revelation 18:4.

In verse eight it states *"Therefore her plagues will come one day-death and mourning and famine. And she will be utterly burned with fire, for strong is the Lord who judges her."* During the Black Death the bodies were burned to stay the plague.

The image of the beast falls to the King of kings as the lion of Judah defeats the lion of Babylon.

THE MARRIAGE OF THE LAMB

The marriage of the Lamb will be at Cana, the place of grace. At the marriage the Lord becomes one flesh with His bride.

The marriage of the bride will bring forth the manifested son's of God in the earth and they will do great exploits under the rule of the King of kings in their souls.

The water of death will be turned into the NEW WINE of resurrected life.

Revelation 19:7-9 *"Let us be glad and rejoice and give Him glory, for the marriage of the Lamb has come, and His wife has made herself ready."*

"And to her it was granted to be arrayed in fine linen, clean and bright, for the fine linen is the righteous acts of the saints."

"Then he said to me, "Write: 'Blessed are those who are called to the marriage supper of the lamb! And he said to me, these are the true sayings of God."

CHAPTER FOUR
RESTORED COVENANT THROUGH OUR JOURNEY WITH JOSHUA AND ELIJAH.

We possess our Promised Land of a free soul through sanctification and belief in the truth.

The book of Joshua and Judges are the instructions on how to inherit the Promised Land.

The Canaanites are seen as the other gods that oppress our soul that must be defeated for us to be reconciled back to our original creation.

Hosea 3:12:7 *"A cunning Canaanite! Deceitful scales are in his hand; he loves to oppress."*

The battles with the Canaanites are seen throughout the book of Joshua and Judges.

There are seven nations of the Canaanites that the Lord promised to deliver us from if we would obey the law and be strong and take back our land. The Lord tells us He is giving us <u>rest</u> and is giving us this land.

The word Noah means, "Rest." Noah and his family were saved from the flood of destruction that came upon the earth. They were placed in an ark of safety that landed in the Ararat Mountains. The word Ararat means, "The curse is reversed."

Joshua instructs us to sanctify ourselves for tomorrow the Lord will do wonders among you.

Joshua 3:8, 10,11 *"When you come to the edge of the water of the Jordan, you shall stand in the Jordan"* (Not yield to sin).

"By this you shall know that the living God is among you, and that he will without fail drive out from among you the Canaanites and the Hittites and the Hivites and the Perizzites and the Girgashites and the Amorites and the Jebusites." "Behold the ark of the covenant of the Lord of all the earth is crossing over before you into the Jordan."

They marched into the Promised Land in obedience and following the Ark of the Covenant possessed the land of other gods.

In the account of Elijah and Elisha we see the journey to a covenant restoration.

Joshua opens with an account of Rahab, the harlot as we are in our worship of other gods. She stands at the beginning of the journey in Joshua by believing the spies (a type of the Holy Spirit). She placed a red cord in her window. We place the blood of Jesus in our hearts window and are saved when the city falls. Her and her family, who were in the house (saved), was later rescued as Jericho fell.

In Joshua 4:15, we read that the Lord spoke to Joshua. *"Then the Lord spoke to Joshua, saying, Command the priests who bear the ark of the Testimony to come up from the Jordan."* They came up from the Jordan and camped at Gigal. Gilgal is the place of the Israelites circumcision and it means, *"This day I have rolled away the reproach of Egypt."*

We now move to 2 Kings 1:2 and discover that this was right before Elijah was taken by a whirlwind of fire into heaven. Elijah went with Elisha from Gilgal and we see the transition from Elijah to Elisha. Elijah means, God Jehovah" and Elisha means, "The God of supplication" "Strength and Almighty" "My God is salvation."

Then Elijah said to Elisha, Stay here, please, for the Lord has sent me to Bethel. Elisha would not leave him and they went to Bethel.

Bethel Jacob called the "Gate of Heaven." The victory over sin begins at Bethel with the vow of obedience to the Lord. Babylon is called the "gate of God" or confusion.

Bethel Elisha was told was the place that the Lord will take away your master from over you today.

Then Elijah said to him, the Lord has sent me on to Jericho. Elisha went along with Elijah to Jericho. Jericho is the place of a spiritual stronghold. It is mentioned in the New Testament where Jesus restored sight to the blind. Matthew 20:30.

The city belonged to the Hyksos period. They were kings of Egypt and can be possibly linked with the Amalekites. There is evidence that the walls did fall as testified in Joshua.

I see the battle at Jericho with the battle between the flesh and the spirit and the wall between our soul and spirit are separated by the Living Word. We cause these walls to fall, as we stay in faith and obedience.

Cursed be the man before the Lord who rises up and rebuilds the city of Jericho after the Lord has set us free.

Then Elijah said to Elisha, the Lord has sent me to Jordan. Elijah took his mantle, struck the water and the two of them crossed over on dry ground. Elisha saw the chariot of fire come and take Elijah and thus he received the double portion of anointing that had been on Elijah.

In going back to the book of Joshua we find that they had to fight at the city of Ai (I is my interpretation as we fight self in this battle).

In Joshua 24 God retells the mighty works that He had done for Israel from bringing them out of Egypt, and defeating the Amorites (lies) and helping when the men of Jericho fought against them. How He delivered the Canaanites into their hand. The Lord said, *"Now choose and put away the foreign gods that are among you, and incline your heart to the Lord God of Israel."*

So the people said to Joshua, *"The Lord our God we will serve, and His voice we will obey."*

Joshua made a **covenant with them** that day, and made for them a statute and an ordinance in Shechem.

Deuteronomy 26:17-18 was used with my walk with the Lord. It is called the vow of Israel and of God.

"Today you have proclaimed the Lord to be your God, and that you will walk in His ways and keep His statutes, His commandments, and His judgments, and that you will obey His voice."

"Also today the Lord has proclaimed you to be His special people, just as He has promised you, that you should keep all His commandments."

Malachi 3:1 *"Behold, I send My messenger, and he will prepare the way before Me. And the Lord, whom you seek, will suddenly come to His temple, Even the Messenger of the covenant, in whom you delight. Behold He is coming," says the Lord of hosts."*

Psalm 50 *"Gather My saints together to Me, those that have made a covenant with Me by sacrifice."*

Hide in a covenant relationship with the Lord, as the Brook Cherith Elijah was told to hide in means, "Covenant."

CHAPTER FIVE

THE BATTLE FOR OUR SOUL

CALLED ARMAGEDDON

The word Armageddon means, Har Mountain which pictures the Mountain of the Lord.

"Your righteousness is like the great mountains."

The battles of Armageddon are the battles for eternal righteousness through the Blood of the Lamb

This is our Giant Goliath battle of who rules our flesh.

Megiddo is a Canaanite city overlooking the Jezreel valley below. Megiddo means, "Cut selves." This explains the circumcision of the flesh, which is now a circumcision of the fleshly desires of our heart.

Jezreel is the valley that the Lord reveals that He will break the bow of Israel in the book of Hosea, the marriage book of the Lord.

"I will betroth you to Me forever; Yes, I will betroth you to Me In righteousness and justice, In loving kindness and mercy; I will betroth you to Me in faithfulness, and you shall know the Lord."

Hosea 1:10-11 *"You are the sons of the Living God' Then the children of Judah and the children of Israel shall be gathered together, and appoint for themselves one head; and they shall come up out of the land, for great will be the day of Jezreel."*

Dagon the Philistine god, had a temple at Jezreel. Dagon falls on his face before the Ark of the Covenant.

The fountain which is Jezreel is called Goliath's fountain, because it was regarded as the scene of Goliath's defeat. Goliath was defeated with a STONE in the head. Goliath is the giant battle of who rules my flesh.

Armageddon will be a seven year period of the cross working in the earth. Armageddon will be the time of Jacob's Trouble. Jacob in Jeremiah 30:7 will be delivered out of it for he will not worship the beast, but stand in obedience to the word of the Lord.

In returning the bride to the original creation, the Lord will bring us to reverse the curse with our choice for God over Satan. He will deal with rebellion, sin and self-love. These are the factors of the fall of mankind in the garden.

The Holy Spirit gave me a revelation as I was studying in the Old Testament. I came across information of events in a seven year period and I saw instantly that these events were to be the events of the end of the age in the purifying of a pure and holy bride.

The fall of Nineveh in 612 B.C, the fall of Haran in 610 B.C. and the fall of Carchemish in 605 B.C.

NINEVEH

Nineveh is a picture of rebellion and called the great city in the book of Jonah. Jonah was told to go get Nineveh to repent. It was a wicked and evil city of Assyria. Assyria pictures the devil in the scriptures.

The book of Jonah gives us many greats in the dealing with the disobedience of Jonah to bring him into repentance. The great wind, the great storm, the great fish captivity is where he cried out to God from the belly of hell. We viewed a great prayer, a great fast, and a great salvation and even a great commission.

The Holy Spirit will do the same in our lives to bring us to the end of our rebellion. Nineveh falls through repentance and self-rule falls to God's rule.

HARAN

Haran pictures the fall of sin, because Haran was the city that had the temple for the moon god cult of sin. Haran means, "Looming up a mountain." Going up the mountain of the Lord is direct implication with that definition. They worshipped sin in Haran.

In Genesis 28:10 *"Now Jacob went out from Beersheba and went toward Haran."* He was walking toward the end of sin.

CARCHEMISH

Carchemish on the Euphrates River (the river of rebellion that flows from Eden into Babylon) saw the final downfall of Egypt. The desires of the world fall from our soul, which Egypt pictures in the scriptures. Pharaoh Necho was defeated, but not until he defeated and killed Josiah, the King of Judah. Josiah was the king that restored the law to his temple and to his life. He died at Megiddo. This pictures our self-death at Megiddo.

2 Chronicles 35:20 *"After all this, when Josiah had prepared the temple Necho king of Egypt came up to fight against Carchemish by the Euphrates; and Josiah went out against him."*

2 Kings 23:29 *"In the days Pharaoh Necho king of Egypt went to the aid of the king of Assyria (devil+ the World), to the River Euphrates; and King Josiah went against him. And Pharaoh Necho killed him at Megiddo when he confronted him."*

Jeremiah 46:2 *"Concerning the army of Pharaoh Necho, king of Egypt, which was by the River Euphrates in Carchemish, and which Nebuchadnezzar king of Babylon defeated in the fourth year of Jehoikim the son of Josiah king of Judah."*

To summarize the fall of rebellion and the lust of the flesh self-rule is repentance. The fall of sin is the lust of the eyes and self-will and falls with the surrender of our will to the will of the Lord.

The fall of the desires of the world fall, as we defeat the false prophet that places a temptation in our soul and brings us to make a choice of which god, self or the God of heaven, we will worship.

The false prophet is the devil as the King of Assyria (2 Kings 6:7 and 2 Chronicles 32:8). Any antichrist in the natural realm will need to come from Syria. Syria and Babylon (Iraq) were the nations that composed the Chaldeans. Chaldea was the last period of Babylon and seen as God's judgment in Habakkuk.

Nineveh was in Assyria and this today is almost in Iraq.

The Holy Spirit spoke to me in 1987 that the "Assyrians are at the Gate."

Self-love Amalek falls with the word of our testimony and choice and our belief in the blood of the Lamb.

Revelation 12:11 *"They overcome him (the red dragon) by the blood of the Lamb and by the word of their testimony, and they did not love their lives to the death."*

REFINEMENT IS THROUGH THE POWER OF THE BEAST, THE DRAGON AND THE FALSE PROPHET.

Rebellion and self-will Nineveh falls from the iron will of other gods. The inability of the saints to obey the law brings them to repentance and a cry to God for His righteousness.

Haran falls as the lust of the eyes in sin with the power of the dragon, that serpent of old. The surrender of our will causes the lust of the eyes to fall from our soul. The dragon is identified as our golden calf of passion and lust. Venus is identified as the dragon planet and Venus is the goddess of love. Venus was also known as Diana of the Ephesians and the city of the Ephesians is the guardian of the temple of the great goddess Diana and the image that fell down from Zeus in Acts 19.

In the study of Og and Sihon the kings of the Amorites, we see these were giants that lived in Ashtoreth, which was the Philistine fertility goddess. Through them, we see that passion and lust fall to the obedience of the law, for these kings were defeated by Moses, before the children of Israel crossed into the Promised Land. Dagon the Philistine fish god, falls before the Ark of the Covenant in 1 Samuel 5:3-

5. Dagon's temple was found in Jezreel and he is the "Beast out of the Sea" in Revelation 13. He is passion and lust on all seven heads of civilizations. He is the Grecian leopard or identified as worldly, and fits the Revelation 17 description of the Grecian eighth beast and the ten kings. Philistines are part of the ten kings and means 'Wallowing." Wallowing pictures loving self and wanting happiness but do not have it. Passion and lust becomes the answer. Depression, self-pity and sickness all come in this package. This empty heart will be restored to the joy of the Lord through repenting and turning to God.

This beast has the feet of the bear which is Media-Persia and pictures the battle between the flesh and the Spirit after salvation. This is a divided soul needing to be made whole in Christ. His mouth was the mouth of the lion which is Babylon self-rule of the flesh and the dragon of passion and lust gave him his power and great authority. The dragon is the devil and serpent of old and the liar to our souls.

The book of Ephesians tells us to put off our old man. Passion and lust is part of our carnal nature. The fall of the dragon restores us from the lust of the eyes to our original creation.

Carchemish is the battle that defeats pride and self-love Amalek. Our self-centered nature falls to repentance

63

because of the false prophet, as he desolates our temple mount and places a sin idol in our soul. He is foreshadowed by Antiochus Epiphanes, as he placed a swine in the temple at Jerusalem and dedicated it to Zeus (and his sexual adventures). Our choice for God over the devil, the false prophet, is the word of our testimony and reverses the curse of the fall. The desires of Egypt fall from our soul, as we are regenerated to a 777.

Beltshazzar in Daniel five was the last Babylonian king. He defiled the temple vessels at the last moment before Babylon fell to Cyrus. The false prophet defiles our temple at the last moment of his kingdom in our soul.

Between these two foreshadows we can identify how he desolates our temple with passion and lust and that this defilement of our soul will bring down Babylon self-rule carnal nature when we repent.

CHAPTER SIX

THE LIVING GOD WILL DEFEAT THE

CANAANITES IN OUR SOUL

The Canaanites were a nation of giant other gods in the Promised Land that the Lord gave to the children of Israel. Canaan is not heaven but in geographical revelation is a picture of our soul. The Jordan River is the type of the blood of Jesus washing over our soul in redemption. The Jordan is a decision of self-death in the believer to turn from sin and follow the Lord. This in turn will result in the Lord giving us rest and a free soul.

The Lord told the Israelites to destroy the Canaanites and take the land. The Lord did not want the Canaanites to pollute the children of God into the idolatry of the worship of other gods. The land of Canaan includes all the land west of the Jordan and Syria. The heartland of Canaan was the costal area from Byblos to Carmel and the Jezreel Valley and the Jordan area. The Jezreel valley is below the Canaanite stronghold of Megiddo.

The word Canaan means, "Merchant." The campaigns of Thutmose 111 extended Egyptian rule into Canaan. We put this together and we have the worldly merchandising as other gods.

Toward the end of the middle Bronze Age Egypt came under the Hyksos (foreign chiefs). The Hyksos were primarily the product of the flowering Canaanite culture. The Hyksos brought in the horse and chariots into Egypt. The Hyksos can be identified with the Amalekites through their king Apop, as related to the Agag of the Amalekites.

Joshua 17:16, 18 *"But the children of Joseph said, "The mountain country is not enough for us; and all the Canaanites who dwell in the land of the valley have chariots of iron, both those who are of Beth Shean and its towns and those who are of the valley of Jezreel."*

Then Joshua spoke to the house of Joseph and said they have great power, but the land shall be yours.

"Although it is wooded, you shall cut it down, and its farthest extent shall be yours; for you shall drive out the Canaanites, though they have iron chariots and are strong."

CANAANITE RELIGION

The virile monotheistic faith of the Hebrews was continually in danger of contamination from lewd nature worship with immoral gods, prostitute goddesses, serpents, cultic doves and bulls.

El the head of the pantheon was the hero of sordid escapades and crimes. Baal was the son of El.

The three goddesses were Anath, and Astarte as the Queen of Heaven in Jeremiah and Asherah who were all patronesses of sex and war.

THE BOOK OF JUDGES SEES THE BATTLE AND DEFEAT OF THE CANAANITES AT MEGIDDO THROUGH DEBORAH THE PROPHETESS AND JUDGE OF ISRAEL.

She sent Barak to Mt. Tabor to fight against Sisera, the commander of Jabin's army. Jabin was king of Canaan.

Sisera gathered all his nine hundred chariots of iron.
And the Lord routed Sisera and all his troops with the edge of the sword.

Luke 2:35 *"(Yes, a sword will pierce through your own soul also), that the thoughts of many hearts may be revealed."*

However, Sisera escaped to Heber's tent where Jael Heber's wife gave him a drink and covered him. He slept and Jael took a tent peg and drove it into his temple.
Judges 4:23,24 "So on that day God subdued Jabin King of Canaan in the presence of the children of Israel.

"And the hand of the children of Israel grew stronger and stronger against Jabin king of Canaan, until they had destroyed Jabin king of Canaan."

In speaking of the battle Judges 5:19 says, *"The kings came and fought, the kings of Canaan fought in Taanach, by the waters of Megiddo.*

How did David kill Goliath? With a stone in the head he killed Goliath. Goliath is the battle of who rules our flesh. The Canaanites are the oppressors of our soul and they go with the sword of the Lord through the living Word and the stone altar of our choice. The Stone altar is a stone in the head of the devil, as the word of our testimony gives victory over the devil of our soul.

THE HITTITES

We have discussed the identity of the Hittites in regard to Jacob and Bethel. Bethel was the old Hittite city of Luz. Bethel is where Jacob turned from his brother Esau, which pictures our flesh desires. We therefore can identity the Hittites as the lusts of the flesh.

In college history I learned that the Hittites were known for their iron production and they developed the secret of iron smelting.

The lusts of the flesh are the Canaanite chariots of iron.

The Hittites are part of commercial Babylon, along with the merchant Canaanites as traders. They are descendants of Heth, the son of Canaan.

The Hittites were a great nation that was located in the whole Syrian region, from the wilderness and Lebanon as far as the great river, the River Euphrates, all the land of the Hittites to the Great Sea, the Mediterranean. The center of Hittite power was in Asia Minor, which was the same area as the Scythians known as Magogites by the Greeks.

Carchemish was a Hittite City and had a man headed winged bull, part man, part lion or bull, and part eagle. This creature was set up by the Hittite kings and Assyrian kings to protect entrances. These are the same faces of the refining fire of the Living Creatures of Revelation 4 called beasts in The King James Bible. These holy beasts are the refining factors of power that bring the child of God to repentance. They are the entrance point to defeat the Hittites.

They transported their gods and goddesses as far west as Asia Minor. Ishtar the fertility goddess of Nineveh and Marduk the head god of Babylon went to the land of the Hittites.

Ishtar is the gate into Babylon that is covered with dragon like animals, and she was Venus the evening and morning star. She was the goddess of sexual love and fertility. Ishtar was the goddess of Nineveh, our identified carnal nature. Again in this information we see that the repenting of passion and lust causes the end of the Babylon kingdom in our soul.

THE HIVITES

They seemed to be in the north and most of their cities around Tyre. Hivite means, "A collection of tents." "Life giver "Chavvah (or Eve), is pointing to the deception of the Queen of Heaven Astarte, who is identical with the Babylonian Ishtar (Venus). She is the Mother goddess, and no doubt Mother Earth and Madonna and Child. Deception will be in the area of passion and lust.

We identify them from the story of Gibeon in Joshua 9:7, 17. They come as deceivers to Joshua. They had rags and moldy bread and pretended to come from far away. They prefer to gain their ends by diplomacy, rather than warfare.

Hamor, the father of Shecham was a Hivite. Shecham is the city that the Israelites restored their covenant with God. Is victory over deception which finally restores our covenant with God?

THE PERIZZITES

They first appear in Genesis 13 as dwelling in the land together with the Canaanites in Abram's day.

The Perizzites and the Rephaim (giants) dwell in the wood country. Perizzites may means, *"a dweller" in an unwalled village."*

They were the original inhabitants of the land. I interpret them as giant sins. Everywhere we are out of the perfect will of God there is demonic activity. This then would be an unwalled village in our soul.

THE GIRGASHITES

The Girgashites are seen among the devoted Canaanite nations only in Genesis 15:21, Deuteronomy 7:1, Joshua 3:10; 24:11, Nehemiah 9:8.

Nehemiah reveals that deliverance from the Canaanites and Girgashites is under the covenant that the Lord made with Abram.

The Holman Bible states the word means, "Sojourn with a deity."

Biblical scholars believe the word Girgashite is associated with the word Gadarenes, which is where Jesus healed the demonic in Mark 5:1; Luke 8:26,37.

In my personal sojourn with the Holy Spirit He had me cast out a demon that was not happy to leave. Therefore I am of the opinion that the demonic control is the identity of the Girgashites.

THE AMORITES

Amorites means, "To say" and it also means, "The high ones."

They were found in the area east of Jordan and the two Amorite kingdoms mentioned in that of Og king of Basham and Sihon king of the Amorites. We have discussed these as referring to the area of passion and lust.

Then in Joshua 7:7 *"Why have you brought this people over the Jordan at all to deliver us into the hands of the Amorites, to destroy us?"*

This is the battle of Ai (I) and it refers to the removal of the accursed thing that they put in their own stuff.

Joshua 7:13 *"O Israel you cannot stand before your enemies until you take away the accursed thing from among you."*

These Amorites wish to destroy us with their lies to our soul. For example we are given the lies and temptation of the false prophet. The devil is a liar and he wishes us to worship him rather than God.

THE JEBUSITES

The Jebusites dwelt at Jerusalem or Jebus before David conquered them and united the city of Jerusalem into a whole city of David.

Jerusalem means, "A holy city of peace."

The Jebusites therefore are the gods of self that are defeated by our desire to obey God. That makes us whole and defeats the Babylonian kingdom of self-rule. *"And they loved not their lives until the death."*

CHAPTER SEVEN

CHRIST COMING TO BUILD HIS TEMPLE

Zechariah 8:3 "I will return to Zion, and dwell in the midst of Jerusalem. Jerusalem shall be called the City of Truth, The Holy Mountain of the Lord of Hosts, The Holy Mountain"

Zechariah 6:12-13 "Behold, the Man whose name is the BRANCH! From His place He shall branch out, And he shall build the temple of the Lord; Yes He shall build the temple of the Lord; He shall bear the glory, and shall sit and rule on His throne, and the counsel of peace shall be between them both."

Zechariah 3:8 "Hear, O Joshua, the high priest, You and Your companions who sit before you, For they are a wondrous sign; for behold I am bringing forth My servant the Branch."

Zechariah 3:9 "For behold the STONE THAT I HAVE LAID BEFORE JOSHUA (1 Samuel 6:14); upon the stone are seven eyes. Behold, I will engrave its inscription, says the Lord of hosts, and I will remove the iniquity of that land in one day."

Zechariah 9:13 "For I have bent Judah, My bow, fitted the bow with Ephraim (Israel), and raised up your sons, O Zion, against your sons, O Greece, and made you like the sword of a mighty man."

Isaiah 32:1, 17-19 "Behold, a king will reign in righteousness, and princes will rule with justice."

The work of righteousness will be peace, and the effect of righteousness, quietness and assurance forever. My people will dwell in a peaceful habitation, in secure dwellings, and in quiet resting places, though hail comes down on the forest, and the city is brought low in humiliation."

WOE TO THE SPOILER OF JERUSALEM (Assyria).

Isaiah 33:1 *"Woe to you who plunder, though you have been plundered; and you who deal treacherously, though they have not dealt treacherously with you! When you cease plundering you will be plundered; and when you make an end of dealing treacherously, they will deal treacherously with you."*

Isaiah 33:9-10 *'The earth mourns and languishes, Lebanon is shamed and shriveled; Sharon is like a wilderness, and Bashan and Carmel shake off their fruits. Now I will arise, says the Lord."*

Isaiah 29:17 "Is it not yet a very little while till Lebanon shall be turned into a fruitful field. Lebanon means, "Heart."

Isaiah 19 "The humble also shall increase their joy in the Lord."

Isaiah 28:16-17 "Behold I lay in Zion a stone for a foundation (the stone altar before Jesus), a tried stone, a precious cornerstone, a sure foundation; whoever believes will not act hastily. Also I will make justice the measuring line, and righteousness the plummet; and hail will sweep away the refuge of lies."

Isaiah 33:14-17 "The sinners in Zion are afraid; fearfulness has seized the hypocrites: "Who among us shall dwell with the devouring fire? Who among us shall dwell with everlasting burnings?" "He who walks righteously and speaks uprightly, He who opposes the gain of oppressions...."

"Your eyes shall see the king in His beauty."

Isaiah 33:24 "And the inhabitants will not say, "I am sick."

The battle with sickness is our battle with fear verses truth. The truth is we are already healed and we must deal with our unbelief in this area.

I John 4:18 *"There is no fear in love; but perfect love casts out fear, because fear involves torment. But he who fears has not been made perfect in love."*

Luke 8:50 *"Do not be afraid; only believe, and she will be made whole."*

2 Corinthians says, *"We perfect holiness in the fear of the Lord."*

Psalm 34:11 reads, *"I will teach you the fear of the Lord."*

DELIVERANCE AND TEMPLE BUILDING WITH THE REVEALED FORSHADOW OF THE PERSIAN KINGS CYRUS, DARIUS AND ARTAXERXES.
THE HOLY SPIRIT, JESUS THE FIRE AND ARTAXERXES THE KING OF KINGS.

The Old Testament foreshadow of temple building in the period of restoration is the plan of eternal temple building in the body of Christ.

In the Old Testament in Ezra 6:14 the temple was completed by the commandment of the God of Israel and according to the command of Cyrus, Darius, and Artaxerxes, king of Persia.

It was finished in Ezra 6:15 in the third day of the month of Adar in the sixth year of king Darius (the Great). Adar is the month of February and March.

I received revelation as I was seeing the dates in Zechariah and Haggai, and Ezra and Daniel. They talked about the second year of Darius and the first year of Cyrus and the fourth year of Darius and I began to ponder the fact that these dates are given and laid out for our purposes. This began my search for the significance of these dates for the end of our age.

Isaiah 44 and 45 led me to believe that Cyrus pictured the work of the Holy Spirit. *"Who says of Cyrus, He is My shepherd, and he shall perform all My pleasure, Even saying to Jerusalem, You shall be built." And to the temple you shall be built."*

"Thus says the Lord to His anointed, to Cyrus, whose right hand I have held- to subdue nations before him and to loose the armor of kings, to open before him the double doors, so that the gates will not be shut: I will go before you and make the crooked places straight."

The Holy Spirit builds the foundation as Cyrus and in the passages of the Branch he also builds the foundation of the temple of the Lord. We of course know that the Holy Spirit is the sanctifier in our temple laying the foundation for righteousness.

What did Cyrus do in historical foreshadow? He was the Persian king that dried up the Euphrates River, (the river of rebellion that flowed from Eden to Babylon.) He was the conqueror that brought down Babylon. He was intent on conquering and the kingdom of Babylon fell to Cyrus and the Persians. (Babylon falls, as our carnal nature and we are made whole). Persia means "divided."

Ezra 1:1 *"Now in the first year of Cyrus king of Persia, that the word of the Lord spoken by the mouth of Jeremiah might be fulfilled, The Lord stirred up the spirit of Cyrus king of Persia, so that he made a proclamation throughout all his kingdom, and also put it in writing, saying thus says Cyrus king of Persia: All the kingdoms of the earth the Lord God of heaven has given me And He has commanded me to build Him a house at Jerusalem (The holy city of peace), which is in Judah (those praising the Lord)."*

Then in Ezra1:5 it said, "*All those whose spirits God had moved, arose to go up and build the house of the Lord which is in Jerusalem.*"

What was the word of Jeremiah that was to be fulfilled?

Jeremiah 3:17 *"At that time Jerusalem shall be called the Throne of the Lord, and all nations shall*
be gathered to it, to the name of the Lord to Jerusalem; they shall walk no more after the stubbornness of their evil heart."

I concluded after finding the Chronological Bible called "Cyrus a type of Christ," that Cyrus pictures the work of the Holy Spirit that will also end Babylonian self-rule in the souls of God's people.

As Cyrus conquered Babylon, the Holy Spirit conquers the flesh. He dried up the River Euphrates and we are told in Exodus 23:29-30 *"I will not drive them out from before you in one year, lest the land become desolate and the beasts of the field become too numerous for you." "Little by little I will drive them out from before you, until you have increased and you inherit the land."*

PROPHETS OF BAAL (LIES) DESTROYED AT MT. CARMEL

When I was working with the signs of the marriage of the bride of Christ I was given a strange revelation of David Koresh and that Waco fire on Mt. Carmel. I had the T.V. on when I heard David say he had a message for the last day church. I went upstairs and my Bible was open to Mt Carmel and the prophets of Baal being defeated by the fire from heaven, as Elijah placed water on the sacrifice. I then looked up the word Cyrus for no known reason except a leading of the Holy Spirit and saw Cyrus means, "Kurush" in old Persian script.

David means, "The Beloved of the Lord." David's message was that the coming fire of the Holy Spirit was to destroy the prophets of lies in a Mt. Carmel experience in the beloved of the Lord, which I had already seen and experienced. David, as strange as it seems announced the coming of Cyrus in 1993.

President George Bush comes in 2000 and in 2001 after 911 fulfilled Obadiah 1:1. He called for all nations to fight evil.

He then proceeded to do exactly what Cyrus did before him, as he conquered Babylon and brought down the king of Babylon Saddam Hussein and freed 50,000,000 people. Babylon is the flesh self-rule, which will also be duplicated in the spiritual realm in the body of Christ. Since everything in the natural is also in the spiritual.

This also fulfilled Jeremiah 25:12 *"When seventy years are completed, that I will punish the king of Babylon and that nation, the land of the Chaldeans, for their iniquity, says the Lord; and I will make it a perpetual desolation."*

Seventy years were completed at the fall of the Soviet Union when the Jews were held captive for the seventy years from 1917 to 1987. It was the time for the end of the King of Babylon.

Saddam also crawled out of a hole in the earth giving us the great sign that the false prophet Cush, the prophet of idolatry was on the way as the Revelation 13 *"The Beast out of the Earth."* In 13:11 He is called *"Another beast coming up out of the earth."* Ancient texts reveal he comes up out of a hole in the ground.

CAMBYSES WAS THE SON OF CYRUS
JESUS WAS THE SON OF THE HOLY SPIRIT.

Luke 12:49 *"I came to send fire on the earth, and how I wish it were already kindled!*

In historical foreshadow Cambyses (Darius the Mede) destroyed all the temples of Egypt not built for the God of heaven. He killed the Apis bull in his Ethiopian campaign.

The Chronological Bible reveals another name for Cambyses was Ahasuerus, the king in the book of Esther.

This shows the victory of the Jew (one circumcised inwardly) over the fire of the spirit of Haman. The spirit of Satan, as the false prophet that wants to destroy God's people. Haman the Agagite (Amalekite) and his ten sons hanged on the gallows built for the Jews.

Victory for the saints is revealed in the book of Esther over the love of self Amalek. The Grecian-Roman power of iron will and the ten kings (horns) that will hate the harlot (lies) and burn her with the fire of the Holy Spirit, as they bring the saints to repentance. Jacob (those that follow the Lord) is delivered out of Jacob's Trouble we read in Jeremiah 30:7. The power of bronze Greece picture other gods and the Roman teeth of iron bring the power of other gods against the clay of the believer and Babylon falls from the souls of God's people. The lies of the false prophet are executed in the fire of the Holy Spirit in a Mt. Carmel choice, of which God is the real God.

I see this time of Jacob's Trouble, as the refinement of the body of Christ, through the fire of the Living Creatures.

We have discussed the fire of refinement seven times hotter than it was normally heated, if we do not bow down and worship Nebuchadnezzar's world image.

Many things happen in the second year of Darius the Great, in Haggai and also the Zechariah visions take place.

The Temple of the Lord is completed in the sixth year of Darius the Great.

The Living creatures of Ezekiel are also seen in Revelation 4:6-7, as the living creatures surround the throne of God. We then find them in the seal judgments in the Revelation sixth seal one through seal four. In Revelation 4 in the King James Bible, they are called beasts and I called them Holy Beasts, for they come from the throne of God and the wheels are full of fire of refinement and they go where the Spirit goes. Their appearance was like the burning coals of fire. Fire was going back and forth among the living creatures; the fire was bright, and out of the fire went lightening.

HOLY REFINING FIRE BRINGS VICTORY OVER THE UNCLEAN SPIRITS OF THE DRAGON, THE BEAST AND THE FALSE PROPHET.

We find the seven days of the Feast of Tabernacles also will be the seven years, as it is restored in the earth. This is the feast of rejoicing and in gathering of the harvest. The fire offerings are sin offerings that follow our surrender to the Lord and they give us peace. These make us burnt offerings before the Lord in total surrender. This is why the road is wide toward God at the bottom of the mountain but it gets very narrow at the top with no turning back for our carnal nature is replaced with the nature of God. He is making us into new creations that will be eternal beings.

THE LIVING CREATURES ARE SEEN AS THE GLORY AND FIRE OF GOD IN EZEKIEL.

The Lion of Judah defeats the Lion of Babylon as the flesh self-rule. Lion of Judah is defined as an altar.

The face of the lion **FIRST BEAST LION** is the king of Babylon, the lion of the flesh and that pictures Cush also known as Bel-god of confusion in the area of passion and lust.

Nergal is "Merodach of war."Jeremiah 50 *"Say, Babylon is taken, Bel is shamed. Merodach is broken in pieces; her idols are humiliated, her images are broken in pieces."*

He is seen as the "winged lion" with hordes of demons. He is the Babylonian sun god (sun to get hotter in the end). He is the god of Pestilence, plague.

FACE TWO "THE BULL" (Calf) Marduk Revelation 4:7) in Ezekiel we see the face as an Ox, but in the Revelation passage it has changed to the Calf.

Marduk, "Calf of the Sun." Ox means "Bull or calf" in *Strong's*.

Marduk is the head Babylonian god and identified with Nimrod, the builder of Babylon. Marduk is seen in glazed tile of the dragon which pictures serpent heads, lions body, and eagles claws, deceit as Nimrod comes as Dagon "The beast of the Sea." Passion and lust falls before the Ark of the Covenant or the Ten Commandments. This is the Apis cult worship with the Venus bull as the golden calf.

Marduk, the bull, mighty in himself and those he commands, is known as Zeus and also Jupiter. Zeus as the bringer of the image is seen in Acts 19.

The golden calf was worshipped at the foot of Mt. Sinai (the foot of our obedience to the law through the Spirit.)

THE THIRD BEAST THE FACE OF "MAN."

Cush comes as Nebo the false prophet of idolatry. He comes as the "Beast out of the Earth." This is found in Revelation 13. He places a temptation in our soul to desolate our temple mount. He had two horns like a lamb, and spoke as a serpent. He comes as the pretender to the Holy Spirit so discern very carefully if what you hear lines up with scripture.

Isaiah 46:1 *"Bel bows down, Nebo Stoops, their idols are on beasts and cattle."*

Nebo is Merodach of trading. Nebo is the god of commerce. Nebo is the god of wisdom in the world and overcoming the world's wisdom to hold for God's wisdom.

Overcoming merchandising is we die to the things that hold us (Romans 7:6).

THE FOURTH BEAST FACE OF "THE EAGLE"

The eagle headed beast of the god of Assyria, which pictures the **devil** Nimrod, Cush's son, builder of Babylon, man's self-rule system.

Ninib is called "the strong one" (Phoenix). The revived Roman power of iron will and iron rule.

We are called to rise above our circumstances as an eagle to receive the victory over the devil of this intense bondage of self-will and love of the flesh is the surrender of our will to the will of the Father at the STONE ALTAR. Our choice for God over the false prophet raises us up with Christ in our victory over the devil.

Ninib is called the "god of iron." Iron Rome is the eagle and Roman iron will comes against the believer in the power of the other gods of Greece to break the clay self-will of the believer. This brings the believer to repentance from self-rule and places them under God's rule and into the great mountain kingdom of God.

This victory over the devil fulfills Daniel 2:35.

Many have taught that these faces are the faces of Christ through the Gospels. *Dakes Study Bible* saw no scriptural foundation for this belief. I had a check in my spirit the two times I heard that, as I saw no basis for that teaching however, the characteristics of Christ are being built into us at this refinement and the strong characteristics of Christ are needed to overcome the fire of the Living creatures.

The third Persian king is Artaxerxes who is called the King of kings in Ezra 7:12, 21. Artaxerxes means, "Kingdom."

"Artaxerxes, king of kings, to Ezra the priest, a scribe of the Law of the God of Heaven: perfect peace and so on."

" And I, even I Artaxerxes the king, do issue a decree to all the treasures who are in the region beyond the River (Jordan River of self-death in God), that whatever Ezra the priest, the scribe of the law of God of heaven may require of you, let it be done diligently..."

Ezra 7:26 *"Whoever will not observe the law of your God and the law of the king, let judgment be executed speedily on him whether it be death, or banishment or confiscation of goods, or imprisonment."* A scary passage in times of judgment!

Ezra 8:22 *"The hand of our God is upon all those for good who seek Him, but His power and His wrath are against all those who forsake Him."*

Artaxerxes pictures the King of kings as the restorer of the law into our temple, as the new heart and new spirit are given to His people.

Ezekiel 36:27 -28 *"I will put My spirit within you and cause you to walk in My statutes, and you will keep My judgments and do them. Then you shall dwell in the land that I gave your fathers; you shall be My people and I will be your God."*

TIMING OF THE TEMPLE OF THE LORD IS SEEN THROUGH THE PERSIAN KINGS.

This is not the time of the return of the Lord Jesus, for we do not know the day or the hour. *The season of refining is seen through the temple building of the Persian Kings Cyrus, Darius and Artaxerxes.*

Solomon is a type of Christ and through 1Kings 7:1 a very interesting fact is seen. It tells us that it took thirteen years to build his own house. In 1 Kings 38 it took seven years to build the house of the Lord. We have two periods here, one seven year period and one thirteen year period to complete to twenty years.

Cyrus reigned eight years following his decree from 538 to 530 B.C.

Cambyses the son of Cyrus reigned seven years from 529- 522 B.C. and the temple building was suspended in

Ezra 4:24 until the second year of King Darius. Temple building was suspended for seven years from 528 B.C.-521B.C.

Cyrus had two sons Cambyses and Smerdis (Bardiya).

After Cambyses went to Egypt the people became evil, so that the lie waxed great in the country.

Cambyses had a dream, which brought a message that Smerdis was on his throne. However Cambyses knew that his brother was dead, so he sent a trusted counselor to kill the imposter. The brother was the living image of the true Smerdis, even with the name Smerdis.

A magus named Gaumata (the name Darius gives him). Rose up in Persia claiming to be Bardiya, the son of Cyrus; he took the kingdom away from Cambyses, and all the people rebelled against Cambyses, until Darius arrived.

Even in history the false prophet's time on our throne is laid out in what is called historical fore-shadow.

Daniel 7:21 *"I was watching ; and the same horn was making war against the saints, and prevailing against them, until the ancient of days came, and judgment was made in favor of the saints of the Most High, and the time came for the saints to possess the kingdom."*

In history this Smerdis is called the "Great Pretender." He pictures the false prophet of a false Holy Spirit that brings lies into our souls telling us to worship the wrong king. Satan wants our worship and only a discerning believer will discern the truth and follow only the true shepherd for the voice of strangers they will not follow.

In the Herodotus account (great Historian) Darius constantly tells the reader to "believe him." There are thirty four instances of the words lie and liar in this text.

Darius speaks of Gaumata destroying sanctuaries as well as confiscating property.

This information was in the book "*The Persian Empire*" by J. M. Cook.

This was great historical foreshadow to the end time desolation of our temple by the false prophet.

Revelation 13 *"And all who dwell on the earth will worship him, whose names have not been written in the Book of Life of the Lamb slain from the foundation of the world."*

TEMPLE TIMING IS IN REGARD TO THE COMING TEMPLE OF THE LORD.
This is not the coming hour or day of the coming of the Lord.

The altar of the Old Testament temple of Ezra in the period of restoration from captivity is restored in 536B.C. Before this time they had been without a temple.

Zerubbabel means, *"Those that have come out of Babylonian captivity."* This pictures the church worshipping the Lord in freedom from self-rule.

We find Solomon had twenty years of temple building with the thirteen years to build his own house and seven years to build the house of the Lord.

In 536 B.C. the altar was established and the temple was finished in 516 B.C. This was twenty years.

Cyrus reigned from 538 B.C. after his decree to 530 B.C. at his death. This was an eight year reign after his decree to rebuild Jerusalem. Cyrus pictures the work of the Holy Spirit.

Cambyses (Darius the Mede) reigned from 529 B.C. to 522 B.C. a seven year period. There was a seven year period in which the temple of the Lord's work was suspended. The work of the Lord's house was being done in the purifying of the bride itself. This is the seven year period that Solomon built the house of the Lord. This period is included in the twenty years to complete the work.

Darius the Great reigned, in regards to temple building from 521-526 B.C. for the temple building started again in the second year of Darius with the Zechariah visions and was completed in the sixth year of Darius.

93

This gives us five more years of temple building from 520- to 516B.C. this gives us 8 years under Cyrus and five years under Darius the Great and we have thirteen years of the Lord building His own house and seven years of the twenty suspended for the house of the Lord to be built.

The twenty years of Temple building are therefore seen in the reigns of Cyrus, Darius the Mede or Cambyses and Darius the Great. Artaxerxes reigns, as King of kings in our soul, as the restorer of the law. Jesus came to fulfill the law not abolish it and He writes it on the hearts of His people.

If the temple started in the first year of Cyrus and ends in the sixth year of Darius we should be able to trace the events year by year as we look to historical foreshadow.

I was told in 2001 A.D. by the Holy Spirit in a song *"It was a new day in the camp of the Lord and to get our temple filled with the glory of My Son."*

I was also told by the Holy Spirit that 1987 was the time of sorrows for the wicked. That He was going to put down all rebellion. I was also told that we were in the time of the "iron and the clay." That was in my spirit for weeks.

In Ezra 1:1 *"Now in the first year of Cyrus king of Persia, that the word of the Lord might be fulfilled, the Lord stirred up the spirit of Cyrus king of Persia, so that he made a proclamation through all his kingdom, and also put it in writing to build the house of the Lord."*

Obadiah 1:1 *"Thus says the Lord God concerning Edom (We have heard a report from the Lord, and a messenger has been sent among the nations, saying, rise up against her for battle.")*

We had this decree from President Bush on Rosh Hashanah in 2001 for all nations to fight evil. The spirit of Cyrus was then raised up by the Lord to fight Babylon (Iraq) and defeat and punish the king of Babylon Saddam Hussein thus, fulfilling Jeremiah 25:12. *"Then it will come to pass, when seventy years are completed, that I will punish the king of Babylon and that nation, the land of the Chaldeans, for their iniquity, says the Lord; and I will make it a perpetual desolation."*

The fall of the Soviet Union ended the 70 years of Soviet captivity of the Jews from 1918-1987.

2001 to 2009 A.D is eight years from his decree and if this is correct as to the Time of Jacob's Trouble with the fire and cleansing of Christ of His bride. The foreshadowed reign of Cambyses should begin around 2008-9A.D. Cambyses destroyed all the idols and temples of Egypt not dedicated to the Lord. Egypt is a type of the world in scripture.

The fire of Malachi is seen during the time of Jacob's Trouble, in which carnal Jacob is brought to spiritual Israel as she wrestles with God.

2001B.C. is the approximate birth of Abraham and we will be seeing the restoration of the Abrahamic Covenant restored in the earth.

Another neat fact David united all Israel after seven ½ years of rebellion. The age of Jacob is seen moving from the age of Esau and rebellion. He fought the Jebusites and united Jerusalem into the "City of David." Here will be the restored house of David after the battle with the kings of self rule, self will, and self love.

JESUS CAME INTO THE TEMPLE IN 8 A.D.

Jesus was 12 years old in 8 A.D. when He went to the temple. Will he come again into his temple in 2008 A.D.? He will first come in His people and He will be indwelling them now. This will be called the marriage of the bride as they become one flesh with the bridegroom.

In 2015 we might began the reign of Darius the Great, the over comer ruling with Christ. In the second year of Darius in 2016 A.D. the drought of Haggai and the Zechariah visions take place in fore-shadow. The temple is completed in the sixth year of Darius, which is 2021 A.D. This is twenty years from 2001 A.D

SHEEP MIRACLE OF PROVISION

I had a sheep miracle experience that told me the white sheep of God will be cared for, during the drought that completes the temple that will bring in the little lost black Sheep. Revelation of this truth made me cry, as I typed the following story for my book.

I was teaching Bible school and the program and what to have the children do brought me to the Lord in prayer and I had a vision of the lost black sheep of Israel and the white sheep coming into the fold. I saw the little sheep in white sheep costumes. I had no idea how to make 23 little sheep costumes by Friday. I prayed, *"Lord if you want me to do this you have to provide the costumes."* The next day a lady came up and asked me if I was looking for sheep costumes and I said I was. She took me to the basement closet and in a box she pulled out twenty three sheep costumes and 1 black costume and one brown shepherd costume, and they fit my third graders perfect. The Lord will provide for His sheep as this was a miracle of provision. This will be the greatest miracle by the Holy Spirit in the earth.

NOAH'S 120 YEARS OF WARNING OF THE FLOOD, AS A PERIOD OF GRACE APPEARS TO BE OVER.

God gave Noah a hundred and twenty grace years before the flood. 1880 A.D. began settlements in Israel and 2000 A.D. is 120 years of warning have been given us.

CHAPTER EIGHT

TEMPLE INSTRUCTIONS

Our first instruction is to be saved and filled with the baptism of the Holy Spirit with the evidence of speaking with other tongues, for we are sanctified (made holy) by the Spirit and belief in the truth.

Jesus said, *"I am the Way, the Truth, and the Life and no one comes to the Father but through Me."*

THE WAY

The Way is receiving Christ into our heart and being born-again from Heaven, with the surrender of our condition before the Lord.

THE TRUTH

The truth is receiving the Baptism of the Holy Spirit, which is the spirit of truth and He brings us to the truth.

THE LIFE

The Life is entering through the veil in death to self and passing from death unto life. We move into the holy of holies, which is the manifested presence of God. He is taking us into the garden of His presence.

My decree from the Holy Spirit was to "Purify and Conquer." Purify by repentance and conquering was standing against my sin, until I was stronger than **my** enemies. I was also told not to commune with the world system on Sunday. I was told not to drink soda and coffee that it all might go well with me. I was told not to fear other gods for the Lord is my healer.

I was told the only way to end shopping addiction was to die to it. We must obey the voice of the Holy Spirit.

In the first year of Cyrus, after his decree to build a house for the Lord and return the Jews to Jerusalem it was also spoken to rebuild the house on its former site, which was Mt. Moriah.

The house shall be built at a place of sacrifices in Ezra 6:3.

Deuteronomy 33:19 *"They shall call the people to the mountain; there they shall offer sacrifices of righteousness; for they shall partake of the abundance of the seas and of the treasures hidden in the sand."*

Mt. Moriah was where Abraham surrendered his son (means, condition) and the ram became the sacrifice. This is salvation

Mt. Carmel is a choice of which God or self to worship. This is redemption when sins are removed.

We are to be washed and ready for the third day we see in Exodus 19, which time I believe has arrived from Christ.

The Lion of Judah brings us to the altar of total surrender. When we lay our life in total surrender we fulfill the stone altar before Joshua (Jesus), and the stone breaks the image of the self-rule system of Babylon off our souls.

We must go to the mercy seat to meet God and ask for His mercy, to bring us into obedience to the law through the Spirit.

We will have opposition from the world all the time we are building our temple.

We are told to prepare the ark for yourselves and your household. Get them saved by inviting Jesus into their hearts and asking forgiveness from the Lord.

Romans 8:13 tells us to put to death the deeds of the flesh by the Spirit and we will live. There is a devouring fire on the top of the mountain (righteousness). Our God is a consuming fire and He consumes our sins, as we want to die to having them.

Luke 9:32-35 says, *"Hear Him"* the angel of the Lord that brings us into the place the Lord has prepared for us we are told in Exodus 23:20.

We are to wash in the laver (Exodus 29) (Leviticus 8:6) for the priesthood of Aaron is to be washed in the water of purification. Cleansing the priests with water refers also to the bride of Christ as priests before God.

Exodus 29 *"And Aaron and his sons you shall bring to the door of the tabernacle of meeting, and you shall wash them with water."*

Become a David, for David reigned over all the desires of his heart.

Build your house through heart belief.

Build our house by truth rest and quickening.

Quickening is the delivering anointing. He quickens who He wills. We are to put on truth to receive this quickening deliverance. Ephesians 6 tells us to put on truth, as the belt of truth, as part of our armor in this evil day. Speak the truth out loud, as faith comes by hearing and hearing by the word of God, until we not only believe in our head but also in our heart. This is putting on the breastplate of righteousness. Take the shield of faith and the helmet of salvation.

Abraham believed God and the plan for eternity and it was accounted to him as righteousness.

Proverbs 11:6 *"The righteousness of the upright shall deliver them."*

Pray in tongues until led to deliverance. Ask the Lord to remove all the lies of Satan from the soul, which is the mind, the will, and the emotions.

Pray the prayer of Samuel, the called out one from the priesthood of Eli.

2 Samuel 7:26-29 *" For thou, O Lord of Hosts God of Israel, hast revealed to thy servant saying, I will build thee a house; therefore hath thy servant found in his heart to pray this prayer." O Lord, thy word is true and thou hast promised this goodness unto thy servant. Let it please to bless the houses of the servant that it may continue for ever before thee and with thy blessing let the house of thy servant be blessed for ever."*

CAPTIVITY

Who are going into captivity? Jeremiah 24 speaks of the good figs and the bad figs. The good figs have been carried away captive for their own good and the bad figs for their harm.

What kind of captivity will it be? It will be situation type fish captivity like Jonah in which there is no way out except repentance. It will be for the purpose of testing our faith. James 1:12 *"Blessed is the man who endures temptation; for when he has been proved, he will receive the crown of life."*

James 1:15 *"Then when desire is conceived, it gives birth to sin, when it is full-grown brings forth death."*

The purpose of their activity will bring the nations to repentance. Isaiah 26:9 *"When judgments are in the earth men learn righteousness."*

Micah 4:10 "and you shall go even to Babylon. There you shall be delivered, there the Lord will redeem you from the hand of your enemies."

CHAPTER NINE

THE FOUR GREAT BEASTS OF

DANIEL REVEAL THE GREAT

HARLOT

Daniel 7 reads *"Four winds of heaven.*

*Matthew 24:31 "They will gather together His elect from the four winds, from one end of heaven to the other,")*stirring up the great sea. "And four great beasts came up from the sea, each different from the other."*

Daniel 7:4 *"The first was like a lion and had eagle's wings. It was lifted up from the earth to stand on two feet like a man."* Here pictures the rise of the image of the beast. The image spreads on eagles wings from Babylon to Rome a possible explanation of the eagle wings.

And suddenly another beast, a second like a bear. It was called to devour much flesh. The bear is Media-Persia and the metal is silver which speaks of redemption. Redemption devours much flesh. The battle is between the spirit and the flesh.

Daniel 7:6 *"After this I looked, and there was another like a leopard, which had on its back four wings of a bird. The beast had four heads, and dominion was given to it."*

This beast was the Grecian beast with the large horn of Daniel nine was the empire of Alexander the Great.

Daniel 9:22 *"As for the broken horn (Alexander died) and the four that stood up in its place, four kingdoms shall arise out of that nation, but not with its power."*

Following the death of Alexander the Great, the world then was all Grecian. It was divided into four parts under four generals. The four generals governed the ten nations or ten kings.

Daniel 7:7 *"After this I saw in the night visions, and behold, a fourth beast, dreadful and terrible, exceedingly strong. It had huge iron teeth; it was devouring, breaking in pieces (into nations), and trampling the residue with its feet. It was different from all the beasts that were before it and it had ten horns."*

Where did it get the ten horns? It conquered all the Grecian Hellenistic territory and now the ten kingdoms were Roman plus Grecian and so we have Daniel 7:19 saying that the fourth kingdom had teeth of iron (Rome) and nails of bronze (Greece).

Daniel 7:8 then mentions another horn or a little horn that has a mouth speaking pompous words. The false prophet is the one who speaks blasphemy into our souls. He plucks up three of the first horns, by their roots. He plucks up Egypt the world, Babylon the flesh, and Assyria (Syria is the picture of the devil). When we turn from the lust of the flesh, the lust of the eyes and the pride of life, it reverses the curse and restores us from the fall.

THE HARLOT IS THE FORNICATION OF GOD'S WORD

Revelation 17 describes her characteristics. She is blaspheming God as a scarlet beast.

The harlot sits on many waters. The waters on which that the harlot sits are peoples, multitudes, nations and tongues and speaks of universal deception.

She is called the "Mother of Harlots" and abominations of the earth.

Not only is she called the great city she is called "Mystery Babylon" for she is the harlot woman of self-rule that has ridden on the seven heads and ten horns of civilizations.

She is adorned in scarlet and purple and scarlet is identified as luxury in 2 Samuel 1:24. Gold, precious stones called great riches of the world system will fall in one hour, for in one hour great riches came to nothing. *"The fruit your soul longed for has gone from you."*

These riches are seen to represent the house of Saul in 2 Samuel 1:24. The house of Saul is a picture of religion that does not teach us to come out of the desires of the flesh. *"O daughters of Israel, weep over Saul, who clothed you in scarlet with luxury; who put ornaments of gold on your apparel."*

SEVEN HEADS

Revelation 17:7, 9 *"I will tell you the mystery of the women and of the beast that carries her, which has seven heads and ten horns." "Here is the mind, which has wisdom: The seven heads are seven mountains on which the woman sits.* Rome is built on seven hills, however mountains refer to righteousness. Psalm 36:6 *"Your righteousness is like the great mountains."* A mountain is defined, "as lifting itself above the plain" and "a bird" *(as rising in the air). Italy is built looking as a foot and Roman iron power is indeed the foot of the image.*

Civilizations that arise in the earth fit this description.

Ten horns are the ten kings that come from Alexander's kingdom.

THE EIGHTH BEAST IDENTIFIED IN REVELATION 17.

In Revelation 17:10 there are seven kings, five have fallen in John's day before Rome.

1 Egypt

2 Assyria

3 Babylon

4 Media-Persia

5 Greece

<u>One is</u> which is Rome, and the other has not yet come, and when he comes, he must continue a short time. Many believe this was the revived old Holy Roman Empire, which was the geographical location of Hitler in Germany.

Revelation 17:11 *"And the beast that was, and is not, is himself also the eighth; and is of the seven, and is going to perdition."*

The beast that was, before Rome was Greece and is not because Greece was conquered by Rome and now is himself also the eighth. Greece is not, but now is included in Rome.

The eighth beast is Roman iron teeth and nails of bronze which is Greece making the eighth beast iron Roman will with the Grecian other gods coming against the clay of the believer.

The ten kings receive power for one hour with the beast.

Revelation 17:14 "These make war with the Lamb, and the Lamb will overcome them, for He is Lord of lords and King of kings."

ALEXANDER THE GREAT BIRTHS THE TEN KINGS.

Alexander conquered the then known world by the age of 33 thus earning the name "Leopard." The word "Nimr" also refers to Nimrod and it means "leopard" as well. Alexander's mother claimed he was the son of the god "Amoun" as she was into the occult.

Daniel 8:21, 22 *"And the male goat is the kingdom of Greece. The large horn that is between its eyes is the first king." "As for the broken horn and the four that stood up in its place, four kingdoms shall arise out of that nation, but not with its power."*

The death of Alexander the king of Greece brought four generals into control of the world.

SELEUCUS

Seleucus took Persia (Iran), Mesopotamia (Babylon) and Syria. Bagdad is called the Seleucia on the Tigris.

Spiritually, we have Iran or Persia as the divided self, the flesh rule of self and the devil rising in Roman iron will with the Grecian other gods.

Antiochus Epiphanes, who desolated the temple in Jerusalem, was a Seleucid king. Antiochus fore-shadows the false prophet and therefore may as well be the natural king of evil many believe is the antichrist. My revelation is spiritual only. A Seleucid king would be from Syria, Iraq or Iran.

The Chaldeans are the last part of Babylon in the Old Testament and they had no interest in the life to come, but a growth in Astral religion, which was the development of a stronger spiritual consciousness. New Age is really old age Babylonian Astral religion.

In the book of Habakkuk the Chaldeans (Babylonians) comes against Judah, but he remembers God's mercy and the power of the saving acts of his God and Habakkuk trusts in God's salvation.

Judah had stubbornly refused to repent of her sinful ways. **God replies that the Babylonians will be His chastening rod upon that nation.**

Habakkuk ministers during the "death throes" of the nation of Judah.

This of course is Old Testament judgment of Judah. However, in the description of foreshadow this applies to the end of Judah (those praising the Lord) in self-death, brought against God's people in chastening.

Habakkuk asks how long this situation will last. God replies that the Babylonians will be His chastening rod upon the nations. This means, "correct, rebuke, take captive." The Babylonians picture self-rule of the flesh, so spiritually this means the intensification of sin to bring repentance from the lusts of the flesh. Habakkuk means, *"One who embraces or clings."* Habakkuk chooses to cling firmly to God no matter what is happening in his nation.

Habakkuk 2:2, 4 *"Write the vision and make it plain on tablets, that he may run who reads it. For the vision is yet for an appointed time, but at the end (of the age) it will speak and not lie."*

Belshazzar, "King of the Chaldeans" was the defiler of the temple in Daniel five and the vision for the latter day is the knowledge of the false prophet, that defiles our temple and we are to hold for God. He was the last king of Babylon.

Habakkuk 2:4 "Behold the proud, his soul is not upright in him; "but the just shall live by faith."

Habakkuk 1:12 *"We shall not die, O Lord, "You have appointed them for judgment."*

The Chaldeans fell to Cyrus in 539B.C. The Babylonians or Chaldeans fall by the power of the Holy Spirit.

LYSIMACHUS

The second general from Alexander's Empire was Lysimachus and he took possession of Asia Minor and Trace. Asia Minor is the home of the Scythian giants. Within twenty years Lysimachus was defeated by Seleucus.

Asia Minor was also the home of the Assyrians and the Hittites.

Seleucus now is the ruler king of Babylon (Iraq) which is flesh self-will. Syria, pictures the devil in scripture and Persia (Iran) pictures divided self, Asia Minor is the home of the Scythians called Magogites in Greece. These picture the giant sins in our head. Seleucus has Trace which pictures religious deception.

This illustrates the package of evil that comes against the saints in the spiritual realm of refinement. We also have Grecian world wisdom and Egypt and her worldly desires.

CASSANDER

Cassander took Greece which was known as Macedonia.

Greece is noted for humanism, the age of reasoning, man's wisdom, sports that are dedicated to Zeus on Mt, Olympus. Passion and lust as the dragon Aphrodite, (she is birthed out of the sea) as the "Beast out of the Sea" with Dagon the fish god that falls before the Ark of the Covenant. Venus is the Roman counterpart of Aphrodite the Grecian goddess of love.

PTOLEMY

Ptolemy, king of Egypt took Phoenicia (Canaan) and Palestine and added it to Egypt. This spiritually places the desires of the world, along with the Canaanites in our soul.

THE TEN KINGS COME AGAINST THE BELIEVER WITH THE EIGHTH BEAST

VICTORY OVER THE TEN KINGS AND THE GRECIAN EIGHTH BEAST GIVES US THE KINGDOM, WHICH IS A FREE SOUL UNDER THE RULE OF THE KING OF KINGS.

Ten kings of ten nations that are divided from the Grecian kingdom of Alexander the Great, who conquered the world, shows us our warfare in foreshadow.

Daniel 8:22 reveal the four generals that took over after the death of Alexander. *"As for the broken horn and the four that stood up in its place, four kingdoms shall arise out of that nation, but not with* its power."

Daniel 8:8 reveals that the little horn comes out of the Grecian Kingdom. Rome conquers Greece in HISTORICAL FORESHADOW.

Daniel 7:23 reveals that the ten horns (horns bring the sacrifice to the altar PSALMS 118:27) or ten kings (nations referred to) come out of this fourth beast, which is Rome. In the putting together of Greece and Rome we have the proof in 7:19, where it reads the fourth kingdom had teeth of iron (Rome) and nails of bronze (Greece). Iron will of Rome is to conquer with the other gods of Greece. Greece has the metal bronze, which means, "fetters and chains or bondage's and addictions."

This intense kingdom of self-rule iron will comes against the clay of the believer. This is the final period of the refinement of the child of God, as we are brought to total surrender. The ten horns persecute the saints of the Most High. Daniel 7:21 reads, *"I was watching; and the same horn was making war against the saints and prevailing against them, "until the Ancient of days came, and a judgment was made in favor of the saints of the Most High, and the <u>time came for the saints to possess the kingdom.</u>"*

1. <u>Media- Persia</u> seen <u>as two horns</u> in Daniel 8:20, pictures the battle between the flesh and the spirit. *<u>The victory involves a daily surrender to the Lord.</u>*

2. <u>Babylon</u> is self-rule of the flesh. The victory comes when we humble our hearts and forsake the world. *<u>We surrender our will to the will of the Lord</u>*.

3. <u>Assyria</u> pictures the devil against our soul (mind). *<u>Ask the Lord to remove all Satan's lies from your mind</u>*. He has to flee when he hears the report of your testimony, as to which God you wish to believe.

2 Kings 6-7 *"Thus says the Lord: Do not be afraid of the words which you have heard with which the servants of the king of Assyria have blasphemed Me. Surely I will send a spirit upon him, and he shall hear a rumor and return to his own land; and I will cause him to fall by the sword in his own land."*

2 Chronicles 32:8 *"With him is the arm of flesh; but with us is the Lord our God, to help us and to fight our battles."*

4. Egypt is a type of the bondage's in the world. *They cried out to the Lord in their slavery and bondage and the Lord heard them and sent them a deliverer.*

5. Phoenicia refers to the Canaanite merchants. The altar of your heart delivers you from the oppressive bondage of the addictions of the lust of the flesh. *Lay them down in surrender before God.*

6.Palestine or Philistine, means, "wallowing" indicating self-pity, sickness etc. *Our belief in the truth and our profession of that truth brings the quickening power of deliverance. Victory over this is repentance of depression, self-pity, loneliness etc.*

7. Macedonia is a Grecian province captured by Rome. Rome is the seat of Satan, as it was moved from Pergamos in 136 B.C. It pictures the accuser of the brethren, and the slander and persecution a believer goes

through. *Our victory is to walk in love, through the power of the Holy Spirit. Ask the Lord to help you forgive.*

8. Greece is worldly wisdom and humanism. It is the age of reasoning and the age of other gods. It is our choice to believe God's Word or the world's wisdom. *Again, ask the Lord to remove all Satan's lies from you.* Be careful to discern the voice of the speaker. The spirit of Anti-christ is everywhere in the world system. The Olympics are from Mt. Olympus and are dedicated to Zeus. I heard on T.V. that Greece is being advertised as the land of the gods.

9. Asia Minor was the home of the Scythian giants. Our giant sins require total repentance and the end of our own struggle and the total surrender to God's righteousness. *"If by the Spirit you put to death the deeds of the flesh you will live"(repentance).*

10. Trace is our tenth king or horn that we need to overcome. Trace is western Greece and in this nation we find Zeus called Baachus, who is known as the "purifier of souls" in Greece. Zeus is associated with passion and lust, so through Trace we find the element for the believer to overcome is deception in the worship of the false prophet and the sin idol or the false image. Number 10 king is the deception placed in our temple mount and number eleven king *makes us come to the choice of which one we will*

117

worship. As the false prophet He places the temptation of choice in our soul. Through the country or kingdom of Trace we can see how the enemy has tried to blind the people to the truth of God's Word. The harlot or false prophet is Cush and he is the God of confusion and we see that the harlot has committed the sin of the fornication of God's Word (Marrying God's Word with idolatry). The god worshipped in Trace was Madonna and child. Mary with baby worship would extend from this. Through the goddess Semiramis, the wife of Cush and mother of Nimrod, she is mother and son worship that was put in place at the death of Nimrod. (*The Two Babylon's* by Alexander Hislop). His death and resurrection as the child in his mother's arms was to duplicate the death and resurrection of our Lord. No where in the Word of God does it tell us to worship Mary. Honor is due her but not worship. Jesus said, *"I am the way, the truth and the life and no one comes to the Father except by Me."* Our victory is to know the Word for ourselves, so we can't be deceived. *Know the truth and the truth shall set you free.*

DRAGON DESOLATES YOUR TEMPLE MOUNT

11. Another horn shall arise after them. This is called the little horn of Daniel and it is, of course, the great dragon described in Revelation 12. The dragon (red dragon would mean sin dragon) that must be overcome by the _belief in the atonement of Jesus and our choice of which God we will serve_.

Joshua 24:15 *"And if it seems evil to you to serve the Lord, choose for yourselves this day whom you will serve, whether the gods which your fathers served that were on the other side of the River, or the gods of the Amorites (lies) in whose lands you dwell. But as for me and my house, we will serve the Lord."*

This choice is required and must be spoken as the word of our testimony to the devil, _as your decision of which God you will worship- self or God. (And they loved not their lives unto the death Revelation 12 11)_.

This choice ends our Babylonian self-rule and places us in the eternal kingdom of life. This dragon is Satan and the devil that is desolating our temple mount with a sin idol.

In the foreshadow Antiochus dedicated a swine to Zeus in the temple at Jerusalem. Zeus is Gog and he definitely wants the believer to worship him and his sin idol image.

Zeus is the chief God of Rome. He is also known as Jupiter.

On June 23, 1994, a rock crashed into Jupiter, which signifies that God is coming, as the "Lion of Judah" (altar of the great stone I Samuel 6:14) to smite Gog. Gog is the

119

leader of the Giants, who is Nimrod, the builder of Babylonian self-rule in Genesis ten. Gog is chief prince of Rosh (means "head") of the land of Magog and they are Scythian giants (*the land of giant sins in our head*).

Man's self-rule will fall to the Lord on the mountains of Israel (righteousness in the spiritual realm), as our giant sins fall from our soul.

Meshech means "sowing of possessions of a precious price" and Tubal meaning is not known, however Tubal-Cain was a smith in hammering all kinds of things in iron and brass. The refiners fall on the mountains of Israel out of our heads (souls) in the spiritual realm. Genesis 4:22 "*And as for Zillah, she also bore Tubal-Cain, an instructor of every craftsman in bronze and iron.*"

The dragon is called Satan and the Devil in Revelation 12 and this gives us the picture of the work of the Dragon. He is the accuser of the brethren and if he is able to lure us into sin with him we will be publicly exposed. The hidden things shall be shouted from the rooftops. Sin is to be judged, for when judgments are in the earth men learn righteousness (Isaiah 26:9). He is also a slanderer, so during false accusations *we need to learn to forgive **and walk in love and victory.***

THE DESTRUCTION OF THE HARLOT

Revelation 17:16 "And the ten horns which you saw shall hate the harlot, make her desolate and naked eat her flesh and burn her with fire."

Revelation 18:4, 8 *"Come out of her My people lest you share in her sins and lest you receive of her plagues."*

"Therefore her plagues will come in one day-death, mourning and famine, and she will be utterly burned with fire, for strong is the Lord who judges her."

BABYLON DESTROYED WITH A STONE

Revelation 18:21 *"Then a mighty angel took up a stone like a great millstone (Asteroid?) and threw it into the sea, saying thus with violence the Great City Babylon shall be thrown down."*

This literal destruction in the time of God's wrath is the natural realm, but in the spiritual realm Babylon falls at the great STONE ALTAR before Jesus.

1 Samuel 6: 14 *"Then the cart came into the field of Joshua of Beth Shemesh (Houses of the Sun), (to be brilliant and a notched battlement), and stood there; a LARGE STONE was there. So they split the wood of the*

cart and offered the cows (our sacred cows) as a burnt offering (total surrender) to the Lord."

THE STONE BREAKS THE IMAGE OF BABYLON

Daniel 2:34-35 "You watched while a stone was cut out without hands, which struck the image on its feet of iron and clay, and broke them in pieces. Then the iron and clay, the bronze, the silver, and the gold were crushed together, and became like chaff from the summer threshing floors; the wind carried them away so that no trace was found. And the STONE that struck the image became a great mountain and filled the whole earth."

Our carnal nature falls to the will of God and we are made whole and restored to our original creation before the fall.

David killed the giant Goliath with the stone in the head. Goliath is the giant of who rules our flesh.

Sisera, the commander of the Canaanites Jael defeated with a tent peg through his head. We put a tent peg through the Canaanites in our soul with our Stone Altar, laying down the lusts of our flesh before Jesus.

CHAPTER TEN

CHRIST COMING TO MARRY HIS BRIDE

Deliverance is by the Ancient of Days as the saints possess the kingdom.

Daniel 7:9-10, 13 *"I watched while thrones were put in place, and the ancient of Days was seated; His garment was white as snow, and the hair of His head was like pure wool. His throne was a fiery flame, its wheels a burning fire; a fiery stream issued and came forth from before Him."*

"I watched then because of the sound of the pompous words which the horn was speaking; I watched till the beast was slain, and its body destroyed and given to the burning flame."

Daniel 7:21-22 *"I was watching; and the same horn was making war against the saints, and prevailing against them, until the Ancient of Days came, and a judgment was made in favor of the saints of the Most High, and the time came for the saints to possess the kingdom."*

"I was watching in the night visions, and behold, One like the Son of Man coming with the clouds of heaven! He came to the Ancient of Days, and they brought Him near before Him." "Then to Him was given dominion and glory and a kingdom."

Revelation 19:7-8 "Let us be glad and rejoice and give Him glory; for the marriage of the Lamb has come and His wife has made herself ready." "And to her it was granted to be arrayed in fine linen, clean and bright, for the fine linen are the righteous deeds of the saints."

1. Christ will come as the Living Word.

2. Christ will take the bride through the Cross to end self-will.

3. Christ will divide the soul from the spirit through the Living Word.

4. Christ will bring forth the Sign of Jonah, as the Miracle of the Resurrected Son is brought to repentance and becomes the "Dove," "the O perfect one" in the Song of Solomon.

5. Christ is coming to bring His pillar of fire and the cloud of His presence to lead His people out of Egypt.

6. Christ is coming as the Lion of Judah to defeat the Lion of Babylon self-rule.

7. Christ is coming to reverse the fall of man.

8. Christ is coming to restore His covenant with His bride in Deuteronomy 26:16.

9. Christ is coming to sanctify His bride and make them blameless before the Father.

10. Christ will restore the House of David. *"I have found David, the son of Jesse, a man after My own heart, who will do all My will."*

11. Christ will change our filthy garments into His righteousness.

12. Christ will transform the bride into the manifested son's of God.

Psalm 81:8-14 *"Hear, O My people, and I will admonish you! O Israel, if you will listen to Me! There shall be no foreign god among you; nor shall you worship any foreign god. I am the Lord your God, who brought you out of the land of Egypt; open your mouth wide and I will fill it. But My people would not heed My voice, and Israel would have none of me. So I gave them over to their own stubborn heart, to walk in their own councils. Oh, that My people would listen to Me, that Israel would walk in My ways! I would soon* **subdue their enemies and turn My hand against their adversaries.** *"*

JUDGMENT ON SIN BRINGS REDEMPTION

In the Amplified Bible in Ezekiel 28:25 we find an illustration of approximate time for judgment to come on the enemies of Israel.

"When I have gathered the house of Israel from the people among whom they are scattered, and am hallowed in them in the sight of the Gentiles, and they dwell in their own land, which I gave to my servant Jacob."

"And they will dwell safely there, build houses, and plant vineyards; yes, they will dwell securely, **when I execute judgments on all those around them who despise them.** *Then they shall know that I am the Lord their God"* *(Ezekiel 28:25,26).*

This sound like it is very close to fulfillment for they are certainly building houses and planting vineyards in natural Israel. They are also saying peace and safety.

The land given to Abraham is spoken of in Genesis 15:18-21.

"Unto thy seed have I given this land, from the river of Egypt unto the great river Euphrates: The Kenites, and Kenizzites, and the Kadmonites, And the Hitties, and the Perizzites, and the Rephaims (giants) and the Amorites, and the Canannites, and the Girgashites, and the Jebusites."

A CLEANSING SPIRITUAL JUDGMENT BEGINS AFTER OUR REPENTANCE. WE WILL TAKE BACK OUR LAND, WHICH IS OUR SOUL, BY GOD'S MERCY.

God's mercy and judgment on sin go hand in hand.

Believer, become a disciple and possess that land that is to be given to you as the heirs of the Abrahamic Covenant. That brings God's judgment on your enemies. If you stay in the Word he will make you a disciple.

They dwell securely when I have executed judgments and punishments upon all those, round about them who have despised and trodden upon them.

They dwell securely after He has executed judgments on their enemies; they do not dwell securely, until He has executed His judgment against their enemies (Ezekiel 28:26). There is a teaching that tells us nothing can happen until Israel is at total peace. Why would God need to come then?

1. **THE CHURCH WILL BE TAKEN INTO A BABYLONIAN CAPTIVITY**.

Micah 4:10 *"And you shall go even to Babylon. There you shall be delivered; there the Lord will redeem you from the hand of your enemies."*

That is the period of the iron will of sin breaking the clay of the believer in order to bring repentance at the altar or Stone before Jesus. When you surrender your will to

God's will, you pass from death into life in experience. You are free and then in resurrection power. This is all done under the leading of the Holy Spirit. You cannot strip yourself or circumcise your own heart. The quicker your will is yielded of course the quicker your struggle is over.

2. THE SWORD OF THE LORD'S MERCY BRINGS JUDGMENT ON OUR ENEMIES (LUKE 2:32).

"And they shall waste with the sword the land of Assyria, and the land of Nimrod at its entrances; (Assyria's own gates). Thus, He shall (the Messiah) deliver us from the Assyrian (representing opposing forces), when he comes into our land and when he treads within our borders" (Micah 5:6).

3. SIN AND WICKEDNESS IS DEVOURED BY THE FIRE OF THE HOLY SPIRIT.

"For wickedness burns like a fire; it devours the briers and thorns, and kindles in the thickets of the forest" (Isaiah 9:18).

4. HE WILL MAKE AN EVERLASTING COVENANT WITH YOU.

"Incline your ear and come to me, hear and you shall live; and I will make an everlasting covenant with you" (Isaiah 55:3).

5. YOU WILL RULE OVER YOUR OWN DESIRES.

He will make you as David, king in your own land or king in all Israel. This passage is only a description or *definition of what being king of Israel means.*

Jeroboam was offered this position in this passage, but he did not attain David's position with God and brought idolatry to the land. He had them give up their trip to the temple in Jerusalem (the holy city of peace), and set up his capital at Shecham. He established shrines at Dan and Bethel. What seems evident in this story is Religion was put in place, rather than a relationship with God. I see this happening in this present hour as religion is fighting the glory and out pouring of God.

Solomon tried to kill Jeroboam, but he fled to Egypt.

The house of David is restored in the earth through you, as David was the "beloved of the Lord."

2 Samuel 3:21 *'Then Abner said to David, I will arise and go, and gather all Israel to my lord the king, that they may make a covenant with you, and that you may reign over all that your heart desires." "So David sent Abner away, and he went in peace".*

6. GOD WILL BECOME OUR TOTAL PROVIDER.

*"And Jacob made a vow, saying, If God will be with me, and will keep me in this way that I go, and will give me **bread to eat, and raiment to put on**, So that I come again to my father's house in peace; then shall the Lord be my GOD" (Genesis 28:20,21).*

We see here a total trust in his care and provision and by this we shall know He is our GOD.

7. WE HAVE TOTAL PEACE WHEN (SOLOMON) CHRIST RULES OVER OUR FLESH BY DAILY SURRENDER..

In the book *the Song of Solomon* we see the love God has for His bride. In the Song of Solomon the bride of Solomon (foreshadow of Christ) is represented by the Shulamite lady. She is taken to his palace in Jerusalem.

Solomon is a word meaning peace and he is a type of Christ and his glory in the temple. We are that coming temple of glory. Hidden in the Song of Solomon is a message for the bride. There are probably many such messages hidden there, but this scripture caught my eye in Song of Solomon 3:9, 10, 11.

"Of the wood of Lebanon (heart) Solomon the King made himself a palanquin (chair).

He made its pillars of silver (redemption), its support of gold (precious saint) and its seat of purple (royalty), its interior paved with LOVE by the daughters of Jerusalem.

Go forth, O daughters of Zion (truth) and see King Solomon with the crown with which his mother crowned him, on the day of his espousals, the day of the gladness of his heart" (Song of Solomon 3:9,10,11).

This is a riddle type of direction or instruction. What lesson do we learn from going back to see how King Solomon's mother crowned Solomon? Solomon is a type of Christ and we need to see how to crown Him King of Kings and Lord of Lords in our soul.

An oath was required or a declaration as to who shall be King on our throne. The word Bathesheba means, "Giver of an oath."

"Assuredly Solomon (man of peace) your son shall reign after me (David), and he shall sit on my throne" (1 Kings 1:17).

The defeat of the flesh rule is by **declaring Christ our Lord**. We need to declare peace is our choice not lusts and cravings from the enemy. In the story this person Adonijah was going to steal the throne away from Solomon (peace from the child of God). He is a picture of what the rule of the flesh is trying to do in our lives. David defeated Goliath in the name of the Lord of Hosts. Elijah is a word meaning, "the strength of God."

We also see the Goliath rule of our flesh fall, as we yield to the strength of the Lord.

8. WE WILL LEARN TO OBEY OUR CONSCIENCE.

1 King 1:34 *"Blow the horn (your mouth) and say LONG LIVE KING SOLOMON"* (King of peace). Our daily surrender to His grace controls the flesh when we are walking in obedience to our spirit's voice, which is our conscience. That verse tells us to confess Christ our victory.

"When He becomes my strength He becomes my salvation" (Psalm 118).

9. SOLOMON, THE MAN OF PEACE, AS TYPE OF THE HOLY SPIRIT REIGNING.

David charged Solomon his SON (condition of peace), saying:

"And keep the charge of the Lord your God: to walk in His ways, to keep His statutes, and His commandments, His judgments, and His testimonies, as it is written in the law of Moses, that you may prosper in all that you do and wherever you turn: that the Lord may fulfill His Word which He spoke concerning me, saying, "If your sons take heed to walk before Me in truth, with all their heart and with all their soul," He *said, " you shall not lack a man on the throne of Israel" (1 Kings 2:3,4).*

Your descendants will reap the rewards of your godliness.

"Then Solomon sat on the throne of his father David; and his kingdom was firmly established" (1 Kings 2:12).

"The wisdom of God was in him to administer justice" (1 Kings 3:28).

10. SOLOMON BRINGS THE ARK OF THE COVENANT INTO HIS TEMPLE OR OBEDIENCE TO THE LAW.

Obedience to the law by the Holy Spirit brings the glory.

"Then the priests brought in the ark of the covenant of the Lord to its place into the inner sanctuary of the temple to the Most Holy Place under the wings of the Cherubim" (glory) (1 Kings 8:6).

The priests, (us the believers) brought in the Ark of the Covenant (obedience to the law through the Spirit.) When the obedience is in the inner sanctuary of the soul, we are under the cherubim of glory. The cherubim are the refiners who bring us into the glory of God.

Romans 8:4 *"That the righteousness requirement of the law might be fulfilled in us who do not walk according to the flesh but according to the Spirit."*

They placed it in the inner sanctuary of the temple on the most holy of holies (our soul, heart). In 1 Kings 8:9 we see what happened when they came into obedience to the

133

law through the Spirit. They made a covenant with God, when they came out of Egypt.

Haggai 2:5 "According to the word that I covenanted with you when you came out of Egypt, so My Spirit remains among you; do not fear!"

1 Kings 8:10 "And it came to pass, when the priests were come out of the holy place, that the cloud filled the house of the Lord."

11. WE WILL TOTALLY SURRENDER ALL REBELLIOUS AREAS. The presence of God or His glory fills the house or our temple as well. Dedicate your temple to the Lord and let the glory of the Lord fill your temple.

12. THE WEDDING AT CANA IS WHERE YOU BECOME ONE FLESH WITH THE LIVING GOD and where He will manifest His glory through you. The third day is the marriage of the Lamb with His church.

On the **third day there was a wedding at Cana**. The word Cana means, "Zealous man FROM CANA" (Canaanites). The word Cana also means, "grace or well favored." This is the first of the signs that Jesus did in Cana of Galilee, and manifested His glory as He changed water into wine. His disciples believed in Him (John 2:11). Galilee was the sea of fresh spring water where Jesus did almost all His miracles. This fresh clear water of Heaven (called grace) meets a zealous man that is turning from his sinful nature of Cana. THE CANAANITES OPPRESS OUR SOUL and we discover the miracle of the wedding has taken place in their lives. The Lord comes as a redeemer, to those that turn from their transgressions. At this wedding in our soul with the Spirit of heavenly grace our death is turned to life or the water is turned to new wine. To explain it further at our total repentance and surrender, we are taken from the carnal state of the flesh to the spiritual state of resurrection life and power.

The third day, as we have stated earlier, is the year which is three thousand years from Christ. I believe that we entered the third day in 2001, as I was given a song that it was a new day.

The wedding took place at Cana of Galilee, which is an enclosed circuit or a circle representing heaven.

What happened at the marriage of Cana? The first miracle happened when Jesus was turning the water to wine. This is the new spiritual wine of the Holy Spirit.

This marriage takes place through the washing of the water of the Word. This washing joins us to the grace of God. Water also symbolizes death and He takes us from death to resurrection life. What happens after the wedding with grace?

13. RIVERS OF LIVING WATERS WILL FLOW FROM HIS CHURCH.

John 7:38"He who believes in Me, as the scripture has said, out of his heart shall flow rivers of living water."

14. DISCIPLES WILL GO FREE IF THEY STAY IN THE WORD.

John 8:31-32 "Then Jesus said to those Jews that believed in Him, "If you abide in My word, you are My disciples indeed."

"Disciples shall know the truth and the truth shall set them free."

15. DISCIPLES ARE INVITED TO THE WEDDING.

> WHO WAS INVITED TO THE WEDDING? JESUS AND HIS DISCIPLES WERE INVITED TO THE WEDDING

(John. 2:1). Who is a disciple? A learner is defined as a disciple.

16. THE COST OF DISCIPLESHIP IS LAYING DOWN OUR LIFE IN SURRENDER AT TESTING.

The cost of discipleship is given in Luke. The opposite of discipleship is death.

Luke 9:23"For whoever desires to save his life will lose it, but whoever loses his life for My sake will save it."

17. THE STONE IS THE METHOD OF PURIFICATION. THE STONE IS THE ALTAR OF OUR HEART THAT OVERTURNS THE LAW WITH HIS MERCY.

At the wedding of Cana we see that they filled six water pots of Stone (could that be like 6000 years of altars), according to the manner of purification. The master of the feast didn't know where it came from, but the servants who had drawn the water knew. The master of the feast called the Bridegroom and said to him, *"You have kept the good WINE UNTIL NOW"* (THE END OF THE AGE).

THE CLEANSING OF YOUR TEMPLE FOLLOWS THE WEDDING!

Christ then cleans your temple. He tells us, *"Take these things away."*

"Do not make my Father's house a house of merchandise." **Canaan means, "Merchants."**

18. DESIRE FOR MERCHANDISE FALLS TO THE HOLY SPIRIT'S CONTROL.

19. THE HARVEST BRINGS IN THE MOUNTAIN OF THE LORD'S HOUSE OF RIGHTEOUSNESS.

Micah 4:1 *"But in the latter days it shall come to pass, that the mountain of the House of the Lord shall be established in the top of the mountains, and it shall be exalted above the hills; and peoples shall flow unto it."*

20. INSTRUCTION TO FIGHT TO GO FREE AS A WOMAN IN LABOR.

Micah 4:10 *"Be in pain, and labor to bring forth, O daughter of Zion, like a woman in birth pangs. For now you shall go forth from the city and live in the open country, you shall even go to Babylon (Intense self-rule). There you shall be delivered. There the Lord shall redeem you from the hand of your enemies."*

21. NINEVEH (SELF-RULE) SHALL FALL WITH A FLOOD OF GRACE.

Nahum 1:8 *"But with an overrunning flood, he will make a full end of Nineveh's very site and pursue his enemies into DARKNESS."*

Zephaniah 3:20 *"At that time I will bring you in, at that time I will gather you, for I will make you a name and praise among all the nations of the earth, when I reverse your captivity before your eyes says the Lord."*

22. THE END OF THE REBELLION AGE OF ESAU TO THE OBEDIENT AGE OF JACOB.

Esdras 5:8 *"Tell me about the interval that divides the ages. When will the first age end and the next age begin? He said the interval will be no bigger than Abraham and Abraham; for Jacob and Esau were his descendants, and Jacob's hand was grasping Esau's heel at the moment of their birth. Esau represents the end of the first age, and Jacob the beginning of the next age. The beginning of a man is his hand, and the end of a man is his heel. Between the heel and the hand, Ezra, do not look for any interval."*

Malachi 1:2-3 "Was not Esau Jacob's brother?" says the Lord." Yet Jacob (Israel) I have loved; But Esau (Edom) (rebellious flesh) I have hated, and laid waste his mountains, and his heritage for the jackals of the wilderness."

23. THE HOLY SPIRIT WILL BRING INTENSE REPENTANCE, AS HIS SPIRIT INCREASES IN THE PEOPLE OF THE EARTH.

Zechariah 12:10 *"And I will pour on the House of David and on the inhabitants of Jerusalem the spirit of grace and supplication."*

Isaiah 19:19 *"In that day shall there be an altar to the Lord in the midst of the land of Egypt, and a pillar at the border thereof to the Lord."*

24. THE FALL OF THE EVIL NATIONS BOTH SPIRITUALLY AND NATURALLY.

THE WORLDLY DESIRES WILL FALL FROM THE HEART, WHICH, IN TURN, WILL CHANGE THE WORLD SYSTEM TO GOD'S CONTROL.

Zechariah 10:11 *"Then the pride of Assyria shall be brought down and the scepter of Egypt shall depart."*

25. GREAT REVIVAL WILL BRING IN THE NATIONS

Zechariah 10:12 *"So I will strengthen them in the Lord, and they shall walk up and down in His name."*

They will be revived in their souls and they will hear God and do His will.

26. OTHER GODS WILL FALL FROM OUR SOULS.

Zechariah 14:20 "In that day there shall no longer be a Canaanite in the house of the Lord of hosts."

27. AT THE PLACE OF BELIEVING THE TRUTH THERE WILL BE DELIVERANCE. Stay in the Word and be a disciple and the truth shall set you free.

28. THE SPIRIT WILL CAUSE CARNAL JACOB TO BECOME SPIRITUAL ISRAEL. REBELLION OF THE FLESHLY AGE OF ESAU WILL PASS INTO THE OBEDIENT AGE OF JACOB.

Obadiah 1:17-18 *"But on Mount Zion there shall be deliverance, and there shall be holiness; the house of Jacob shall possess their possessions. The house of Jacob shall be a fire, and the house of Joseph a flame; But the house of Esau shall be stubble; they shall kindle them and devour them, and no survivor shall remain of the house of Esau, for the Lord has spoken."*

The great River Euphrates is a picture of rebellion out of the Garden of Eden, flowing through Babylon.

The River Euphrates WILL DRY UP.

29. REBELLION TO BE OVERCOME, LITTLE BY LITTLE IN GOD'S PEOPLE.

The great Cyrus of Persia stopped the water little by little and took the city of Babylon.

The Holy Spirit, as well, will stop the river of rebellion little by little, one craving, one lust, one sickness at a time.

We see in Revelation 16:12 that the river Euphrates is dried up in the natural realm. The following description of the spiritual powers involved in this last battle is truly awesome.

Revelation 16:12-14 *"Three unclean spirits like frogs coming out of the mouth of the dragon, out of the mouth of the beast, and out of the mouth of the false prophet. For they are spirits of demons, performing signs, which go out to the kings of the earth (those ten kings of Greece which is now Rome) and the whole world to gather them to the battle of that great day of God Almighty."*

30. FORCES OF DARKNESS WILL BE RELEASED IN JUDGMENT OF THE EARTH. THE RESULT WILL BE DECEPTION AND DEATH OR REPENTANCE AND TOTAL SURRENDER, BRINGING ETERNAL LIFE!

Revelation 9:15 *"Loose the four angels which are bound in the great River Euphrates."*

David defeated Syria (Anti-christ dragon) to recover his territory at the River Euphrates (river of rebellion) (2 Samuel. 8:3).

Egypt (The world) and Assyria (devil) came against God fearing king Josiah and caused his death at the River Euphrates (2 Chronicles. 35:20). This is a picture of death to the law at the River Euphrates, as mercy triumphs over judgment.

31. MAN'S SELF-RULE IS OVER WAS SPOKEN DIRECTLY INTO MY SPIRIT.

Babylon shall sink, as a stone in the River Euphrates,

"Thus Babylon shall sink and not rise from the catastrophe that I will bring upon her" (Jeremiah 51:64).

32. THE DESTRUCTION OF THE WICKED IN THE DAY OF HIS WRATH.

Jeremiah 46:10 "For this is the day of the Lord God of Hosts, a day of vengeance, that He may avenge Himself on His adversaries, the sword shall devour; it shall be satiated and made drunk with their blood; for the Lord God of Hosts has a sacrifice in the north country by the River Euphrates."

I was looking at a picture of Noah's Ark sitting on top of Mt. Ararat in Armenia.

The ark landed on top of Mt. Ararat in Armenia, when I realized that the Scythian giants were from the Caucasus area. This is below Mt. Ararat. Armenia and the Hittite area are known for iron production. They sold it to Greece and also to Carchemish. We have pictured, in the natural realm the iron giant strongholds that hold us in bondage to the lusts of the flesh. At the defeat of the iron will of the Hittite giant lusts of the flesh pictured in Asia Minor and the iron of commercial idols of Carchemish, a Hittite capital you get in the ark on top of Ararat. Ararat means, "The curse is reversed," as we have chosen for God over Satan and his temptations.

Nineveh pictures the fall of self-rule in our soul. The fall of Haran pictures the fall of sin from our soul and the fall of Carchemish pictures the fall of the idols and temples in Egypt. Cambyses destroyed all the idols of Egypt and He is also known as Darius the Mede.

In foreshadow type Mede is the believer that has inherited the kingdom and is overcoming his sinful nature. (Media contained rebellious Nineveh). The seven years of temple building under Darius the Mede, known as Cambyses, will be the workings of the cross in the earth.

CHAPTER ELEVEN

SUMMARY AND REVIEW OF THE

MATERIAL

"TEACH MY PEOPLE HOW TO FIGHT AMALEK"
AMALEK IS OUR SELF-CENTERED MAN.

Amalek is our love of self carnal nature revealed as the flesh, as identified through Amalek, as Esau's grandson. Through the twin sons of Isaac, who is the child of promise, we see the picture of what path we as Christians are required to take to receive eternal life.

Two nations were in the womb of Rebekkah in Genesis. Two nations will be separated from the twin sons of Jacob and Esau.

Jacob was obedient and followed after his eternal birthright of his father. We also must be obedient and follow after our eternal birthright of our heavenly Father.

Esau on the other hand gave up his birthright for a bowl stew. This was a separation not because he was hungry, but because he so easily traded eternity for the temporal pleasures of the flesh.

The final separation of the nations will be through the testing of the image of the beast and the temptation of the false prophet. This temptation will be the dragon, which is identified as passion and lust for the people and things of the world system.

We see this separation in Matthew 13:30 *"Let both grow together until the harvest, and at that time of harvest I will say to the reapers, "First gather together the tares and bind them in bundles to burn them, but gather the wheat into My barn."*

OUR JOURNEY HOME TO MATURITY

Our journey in the Christian life is progressive. It begins in our acceptance and of the forgiveness of our sins through the work of the cross. It moves from the new birth with the new nature to the glory of His perfection.

Our journey begins in our repentance and turning from sin to the righteousness of Christ.

Isaiah 26:9 *"When Your judgments are in the earth, the inhabitants of the world will learn righteousness."*

The book of Joshua is the book of sanctification. It is the counter book to the book of Ephesians that tells us to put off our old man.

Our journey involves bringing back the ark of obedience into our temple, as David brought the Ark of the Covenant into his temple at Jerusalem.

Bringing the Ark back means coming into obedience to the law, through the deliverance of the Holy Spirit.

Our journey to righteousness is revealed through the journey the children of Israel took to inherit the Promised Land, which is a free soul.

The Israelites went from the Jordan, which is a death to self-decision to Gilgal, the place of the circumcision. On this side of the cross circumcision is of the heart. They went to Jericho, which is the defeat of our Canaanite strongholds of sin. In Jericho the faith of Rahab, the harlot (away from God), stands at the door of the Promised Land. She said, *"According to your words so be it."* She believed the spies (Holy Spirit) as Jacob had done at Bethel with his vow to obey and trust God. She placed the scarlet cord (blood of Jesus) in her window.

We also can see a similar journey that Elijah took with Elisha into the power of the double portion anointing.

The Israelites have victory over Ai (I) at the second attempt and death to self-love, as the (sword of the Lord) spear of Joshua utterly destroyed all the inhabitants of Ai. This is the separation of our soul from our spirit.

147

Israel then became a worshipper of the Lord and offered burnt offerings and sacrificial peace offerings to the Lord. (These appear to be sin offerings to clean our house from sin). Our God is a consuming fire.

Israel renews the covenant to the Law of Moses. We receive obedience to the Ten Commandments, through Jesus fulfilling the law in us and writing the law in our heart.

There are three stages in our journey to spiritual maturity.

1. To be washed in the blood of Jesus. Mt. Moriah is salvation with new life of the spirit within.

2. The putting off our old nature through the cross of Christ is with the surrender of our will to the will of God.

3. The receiving of the Baptism of the Holy Spirit, is the power to overcome sin, for we are sanctified by the Holy Spirit. The putting off of the sin that so easily besets us is through the refining fire and our deeper surrender for redemption of the root of sins. Final victory will be over death and the total redemption of our bodies.

THE FEASTS REVEAL OUR JOURNEY TO REDEMPTION

Passover signifies being born-again and pictures the exodus from Egypt, the desires of the world.

Pentecost is the experience of being filled with the Holy Spirit and speaking with other tongues, as they did in the upper room in Jerusalem when tongues of fire fell on the disciples and they spoke with other tongues.

Yon Kippur, as the time of repentance, will be restored in the earth with the coming of the Lion of Judah.

The Feast of Tabernacles is the final stage of Redemption. This brings us to final maturity in Christ.

The final fullness of our redemption and the veil of our flesh no longer hides the glory of Christ in us. The fullness of God is being filled with His love.

Paul speaks of *"Christ in you the hope of glory." Colossians 1:27.*

BUILD OUR HOUSE FOR THE LORD

We build our house by the fall of Babylon self-rule. Babylon is the kingdom of gold and gold lies over the temple mount in Jerusalem. They cannot build their temple in Jerusalem, because the dome of the Rock lies over the temple mount. We cannot build our temple for the Lord, until self-rule is off our temple mount in our soul.

We must build our house with sanctification and by belief in the truth, by heart belief. Build your house by confession in captivity, by quickening of illuminations of the truth.

We build it on the original site of Mt. Moriah in total surrender of our condition, as we purify and conquer.

We build our house, as we wash our clothes with fire and water and death to our sin and put away all foreign gods.

We build our house by the Living Word separating our soul from our spirit, as we renew our mind.

Build by wearing the armor of righteousness, peace and the helmet of salvation, which is a soul that is saved by being washed in the blood. This called the renewal of our mind. Build by taking the sword of the Spirit which is the Word of God. Stand in the evil day with the shield of faith.

Build your house on the finished work of the cross. Build your house into Solomon's temple of glory.

Build your house by turning from brother Esau in repentance. Build your house by the crucifixion of self death in total surrender at the cross. Jesus taught us to go through the cross by *"Not My will but Yours be done"*

Build your house by the instructions in Joshua.

Meet God at the Ark of the Testimony above the mercy seat and receive His mercy to obey the law of the Ten Commandments.

Obey the Angel of the Lord revealed in Exodus 23:20. We are to hear Him and obey Him.

Destroy the "Dreamer of Dreams" in Deuteronomy 13 who is to test us and see if we obey the Lord. He pictures the false prophet. Speak your testimony over the sin idol he places in your soul. Ask the Lord to remove all Satan's lies from your soul and pray in tongues until breakthrough comes. Take every thought captive to the obedience of Christ, which is an important issue in the coming spiritual warfare of the bride to become an over-comer. This can be accomplished when the mind has been renewed.

Build your house and be found blameless through our faithfulness, during the trials of the three battles of Armageddon, which are the battles for eternal righteousness.

Fasting will be required to receive your ministry! You will be told for how long. Discern the spirits carefully that they line up with the word.

We are told in Romans 7:6 that we need to die to the things that hold us. And some the fire of God will consume, when the water of death is placed upon the sin offering.

Restore our covenant with the king through Deuteronomy 26:16.

Zechariah 1:16 *"I am returning to Jerusalem with mercy, My house shall be built in it, says the Lord of hosts."*

OPENING UP THE BOOK OF DANIEL

We open Daniel and find God's people in captivity in Babylon. This pictures the place of self-will in our lives.

Daniel opens and he sees the end of the captivity following the seventy years of captivity. We have seen the same end after seventy years of God's people held captive in the Soviet Union from 1917-1987.

We see an image is setup by Nebuchadnezzar, the king of Babylon. He wants God's people to bow down and worship this image. When they will not bow down and worship this image they are thrown in the fire of refinement, where the fire of the intensity of the sin is turned up seven times hotter than it normally was.

In Daniel we see that God sent His angel to deliver the friends of Daniel through the fire, because they trusted in Him and frustrated the king's word, and believed God's word and would not worship any god, but their own God.

We see in Daniel the image as the world system, and the fire of refinement.

We also see the four beasts that arise in the earth and the Grecian kingdom of Alexander the Great, as the large horn.

We understand that the ten kings come from the Grecian kingdom and these are the refining factors in the purification of the bride of Christ.

We see the humbling of the king of Babylon, our flesh self-rule for seven years. We see the defilement of the temple vessels before deliverance comes from Cyrus to end the nation of Babylon.

We see the stone that is laid over the mouth of the lions den that delivers Daniel from the lions. Babylon's animal is the lion (self-rule of the flesh.) The stone altar before Jesus (Joshua) is seen in 1 Samuel 6:14.

We see deliverance of the Ancient of Days and we see the fore shadow of the little horn as Antiochus Epiphanes that dedicated the temple in Jerusalem to Zeus by putting a swine on the altar.

We learned that the first year of Darius is the time for God's people to come out of Babylonian captivity. This is Darius the Mede or Camybses, because it reveals he is the son of Ahasuerus, which is also Cyrus. Ahasuerus is the king in the book of Esther.

We see the time of the end of sin in Daniel 9 at seventy weeks of years. 62 weeks plus 7 weeks to equal 69 weeks at the time messiah is cut off. This leaves another seven years to end sin and transgression. This seven year period is the Time of Jacob's Trouble, in which Jacob will be delivered and washed in the blood.

In Daniel 11 we discover the battle between Persia and the rule of Greece. This spiritually is our divided self dealing with the Bronze of Greece, which means, chains and fetters or addictions and bondages.

This battle is seen in historical foreshadow of Egypt, as the king of the south (world) and Syria, the king of the North, which signifies the devil. Our battle as a divided soul wages warfare with the devil and the world desires and the other gods of Greece and worldly wisdom. Victory makes us whole in our soul.

Zechariah 9:13 *"And raised up your sons, O Zion, against your sons, O Greece, and made you like the sword of a mighty man."*

Daniel 11:36 is the story of the "Willful King." This identifies the false prophet and the desolations and deliverance out of the time of Jacob's Trouble.

BABYLON FALLS AS OUR SELF-RULE FALLS, AT OUR MT. MORIAH

WE DEFEAT THE KINGS MOSES DEFEATED THROUGH OBEDIENCE TO THE LAW THROUGH THE MERCY OF CHRIST.

Moses defeats the Amorite kings of Ashtoreth, Og and Sihon, on the east side of the Jordan. These kings illustrate for us passion and lust. These kings ruled half of Gilead and that means, *"To have affection for sexually or otherwise."*

Before we cross the Jordan in self-death we must be bumped up against the law, of Moses. Moses illustrates for us the deliverer out of Egypt. He brought the people out of Egypt by great judgments. They crossed the Red Sea, which pictures the sin sea in the spirit. When we come out of Egypt it is called Gilgal in the journey with the Israelites. Gigal means, "The reproach of Egypt is rolled away. It pictures salvation and forgiveness of sin.

It is at our Mt. Moriah where we surrender our condition before the Lord and cry out for deliverance. What was their position in Egypt, but slavery and bondage? How were they finally delivered by Moses? They cried out for mercy in their slavery and God sent them a deliverer. We also have to cry to God for mercy and know we can not be righteous on our own. Moses and the Ten Commandments give us our deliverer out of Egypt as well. When we receive Christ we are in position righteous, however, but now we become experientially righteous. This is not sinless perfection, for when we sin He is faithful and just to forgive our sins.

Babylon is the world system of man's self-rule in the three part world system of political, commercial and religious systems.

The fall of Adam involved the lust of the flesh, the lust of the eyes and the pride of life. When the curse is reversed it will be the Spirit ruling the soul and the self-centered man will be overthrown.

Genesis 3 *"So when the woman saw that the tree was good for food, that it was pleasant to the eyes, and a tree desirable to make one wise she took of it s fruit and ate. She also gave it to her husband with her and he ate."*

1 John 2:16 *"For all that is in the world- the lust of the flesh, the lust of the eyes, and the pride of life is not of the Father, but is of the world."*

When we surrender to the rule of God in our passions and lusts our carnal nature comes under the rule of God. We are then brought to a place of Bethel, where we as Jacob did vow to obey God with his aid and mercy if God will take care of us. Our Nineveh or rebellion of the lust of our flesh has fallen to God, as Nineveh was called to repent by Jonah. They repented and judgment was halted.

Babylon is also sins and the lust of the eyes then must fall by the surrender of our will to the will of the Lord. We are called "to purify and conquer." We have purified by repentance and now are called to conquer which means to hold against sin, taking every thought captive to the obedience of Christ. Little by little the Holy Spirit also referred to as the Angel of the Lord, delivers us and puts our sin under His feet.

Babylon is also the religious deception of the flesh and knowing the truth of the Word sets you free of deception. We are brought to a choice in possession of our Promised Land, as to who we will worship Satan or God, self-love or the God of heaven. Our choice for God delivers us out of the Babylon kingdom and reverses the curse of the fall. Religious Babylon falls as this Mt. Carmel choice brings us to the light of truth.

Mt Carmel is redemption as the root of sin is removed. Mt. Carmel is the choice Elijah had with the prophets of Baal (lies). He put water (of death) on the sin sacrifice and heaven came and consumed the sacrifice.

They overcame him (the dragon of deceit who is the false prophet) by the word of their testimony and the blood of the Lamb and they loved not their lives unto the death.

POSSESS OUR PROMISED LAND

We possess our Promised Land of a free soul with the Angel of the Lord, as the fall of Babylon our self-rule falls by repentance in the fire of God. Our Promised Land is taken with the defeat of the Canaanites (other gods in our soul). We are told that the Living God well without fail deliver us from the Canaanites that oppress our soul (mind, will, and emotions).

We possess our Promised Land as we look to the instructions in the book of Joshua. We have stated that the book of Joshua is the accompanying book to the book of Ephesians, which tells us to put off our canal nature of the old man. Putting off our old man is putting to death by the spirit our carnal nature.

Romans 8:13 *"If by the Spirit you put to death the deeds of the body you will live."*

We are told to be strong and courageous. We are told to meditate day and night in the Word, so as not to miss the time of your visitation of the Living Word. The Living Word separates our souls from our spirit and brings us back to our original creation.

We are told to stay in the word that we might observe to do all that is written in the law.

Revelation 22:14 *"Blessed are those that do His commandments, that they may have a right to the Tree of Life."*

The separation of our soul from our spirit must take place for us to pass through the flaming sword of the cherubim that guards the tree of life. We must pass through the veil that separates death from life. *"When one turns to the Lord the veil is taken away."*

We are told to Arise and go over the Jordan and be cleansed in our soul from Adam to the Dead Sea. We are told to sanctify ourselves so the Lord will do wonders among you tomorrow. We are told we will cross the Jordan on dry ground.

We possess the Promised Land through the judgments of God's chastisements.

Psalm 94:12 K. J. *"Blessed is the man whom the Lord Chastenest."*

The Book of Jonah reveals God's dealing with man to bring mankind into doing His will.

The book of Jonah has 9-10 greats listed as the Great City of Nineveh, Assyria (Self-will in the soul started by Nimrod in Genesis 10.) I just heard on T.V. today that they found in Iraq the crown of Nimrod and the crown of the queen of Assyria. A confirming sign to me that Nimrod and his image is about to be built in the souls of God's people and then will fall at our choice. The image of the beast is on the horizon. Saddam Hussein crawled out of a hole, predicting the coming false prophet Cush, who is the god of confusion.

Nineveh is the home of the "hidden god" Ninus. He is the god of our carnal nature. But he is about to fall from the people of God.

Nineveh is called wicked by God and He tells Jonah to get Nineveh to repent. This is similar to the command of Cyrus (The Holy Spirit) to build our house by purifying and conquering. This appeared on almost every page of my bible as the Lord came to me as the Living Word. The Lord rises up the spirit of Cyrus (the anointing) to build the house of the Lord.

The Book of Jonah reveals that God send a great wind (Power of the Holy Spirit) with a great storm. We hear of a great fish that Jonah was placed in and that signifies a great captivity of the fire of sin, which brings a great repentance.

The great repentance brings a great deliverance. A great humbling of Nineveh will bring a great harvest of souls, and in the book of Jonah God then relented of doing harm to Nineveh.

Matthew 12:41 *"The men of Nineveh will rise in judgment with this generation and condemn it, because they repented at the preaching of Jonah; and indeed a greater than Jonah is here."*

THE ISRAELITES FIGHT THE CANAANITES TO INHERIT THE LAND.

When the children of Israel had defeated the Kings Og and Sihon through Moses they then had crossed the Jordan with Joshua. We can only go so far with the law and the grace of Christ is pictured with Joshua. He takes over to cleanse our soul and deliver us from our enemies the Canaanites.

When the kings of the Amorites who were on the west side of the Jordan, and all the kings of the Canaanites who were by the sea heard that the Lord had dried up the waters of the Jordan from before the children of Israel until we had crossed over, the Canaanites feared Israel.

However, following the victory of Ai in Joshua 9 the Canaanites gathered together to fight Joshua (Type of Jesus) with one accord.

We see deception of the Hivites, lies of the Amorites. All these kings and their land Joshua took at one time, because the Lord God of Israel fought for Israel.

The land that remained to be fought was Philistines (wallowing self-pity, depression, fear, loneliness etc.)

The land of the Geshurites appear to be demonic oppressors in our sojourn with the Holy Spirit. He leads us in deliverance to demonic control. They mean, "Sojourn with the deity." The word Gadarenes refer to the same people and that is where Jesus cast out the demonic.

THE FIGHT TO POSSESS OUR SOUL, A PROMISED LAND OF PEACE.

How did they fight? In Judges 3:9 we find they cried out to God and Nehemiah 9 said they separated themselves unto God, and Deuteronomy 8:2 said they remembered the blessings of God in their lives. Deuteronomy 7 reminds us to keep the commandments and repent where we don't line up. It is a command to conquer Canaan. Purge evil from the midst of you and rejoice in the Lord in Deuteronomy 18. Walk in His ways and cleave unto Him in Deuteronomy 11:22. Proclaim God King in Numbers 10:9.

Descendants of Abraham were called to act by similar faith and walk in the same obedience unto God. The Jordan must be crossed and cities captured and the battles must be fought before Israel could possess their inheritances. God had promised to deliver them and us from the Canaanites that possess our soul.

RESTORE OUR COVENANT WITH THE KING

When we have possessed our promised land of a freed soul the Lord will bring us into a covenant relationship.

Joshua 16:17 *"And Joshua spoke to the house of Joseph- to Ephraim and Manasseh saying "You are a great people and have great power; you shall not have one lot only. But the mountain country shall be yours. Although it is wooded you shall cut it down, and its farthest extent shall be yours; you shall drive out the Canaanites they have iron chariots and are strong."*

Joshua 15:63 *" The Jebustites, the inhabitants of Jerusalem, the children of Israel could not drive out, but the Jebusites dwell with the children of Judah to this day. The kings of self were conquered by David and came into unity making Jerusalem, the holy city of David."*

THE RENEWAL OF THE COVENANT AT SHECHEM

Joshua gathered all the tribes of Israel to Shechem and called for the elders of Israel for their heads for their judges, and for their officers; and they presented themselves before God.

In Joshua 24, Joshua prophesied of all the deliverances God had done for the children of Israel like bringing them out of Egypt. How He gave the Amorites into their hands. How He defeated the men of Jericho, as they fought against them, and how He delivered the Canaanites (oppressors of our soul) into their hands.

At this place in God we are brought to choose which God or love of self we will worship. Joshua 24:15 *"Now choose for yourselves this day whom you will serve, whether the gods which your fathers served that were on the other side of the River, or the gods of the Amorites (lies) in whose land you dwell." "But as for me and my house we will serve the Lord."*

Joshua 24:25-26 "So Joshua made a covenant with the people that day, and made for them a statue and an ordinance in Shechem."

Then Joshua wrote these words in the Book of the Law of God. And he took a LARGE STONE, and set it up there, under the oak that was by the sanctuary of the Lord. The large oak pictures the tree of Life. We come into life with the large stone altar before Jesus, as He restores us to a covenant relationship by bringing us into Life. *"You will live not die."*

THE MARRIAGE OF THE BRIDE OF CHRIST

Hosea 2:19-20 *"I will betroth you to me forever; yes I will betroth you to Me. In righteousness and justice, in loving kindness and mercy; I will betroth you to Me in faithfulness, and you shall know the Lord."*

The bride and groom become one flesh at the marriage, during the restored Feast of Tabernacles in the earth.

The bride will pass through the veil from death unto life as the veil separated the two, the holy place from the holies of holies.

The veil is removed at the wedding and the groom kisses the bride. Song of Solomon *"Let him kiss me with the kisses of his mouth."* This implies a very intimate relationship being established between the Lord and His bride.

The wedding will take place in Cana, the place of grace and favor. This is where the water of death is turned into the new wine of resurrected life. We are in our new wineskins.

Marriage of Christ takes place as He indwells His bride at her total surrender of her life. He marries her at her choice for God over the image of the Beast and when she has laid down her life, as they loved not their life unto the death (to self spiritually). Many have no doubt done this physically as well.

In the revelation from 1 Kings 17 we find that the soul is revived and His children are brought back to hearing and doing the will of God.

Once the Lord has indwelt His beloved she will rule and reign with Christ. We see this with David that he was now king in all Israel and king over all the desires of his heart and did all God's will.

In the holy of holies we find the Ark of the Covenant, which contains the Ten Commandments. We need to go to the mercy seat on top of the Ark of the Covenant also called the Ark of the Testimony. This is where God meets with us and His mercy and His righteousness come when we humble ourselves before Him and where we do not line up with the word of God we ask for His righteousness, as we are ready to die to the sin.

A NEW WEDDING GARMENT ON THE NIGHT OF MY WEDDING.

I had an experience with my wedding gown at my own wedding, as my wedding garment was delivered to the wrong church. The bridal shop came and brought me the most beautiful garment in the store, as they had failed to deliver my dress to the correct church.

Years later, I went to my husband's home town to minister with my husband and I met the lady that had made my wedding cake. I was speaking on the marriage of the Bride of Christ at our meetings. Seeing this lady recalled my wedding with the strange events of my dress. Now spiritually, the Lord had just taken me through the wedding and brought me to repentance and reconciled me to the God of the Universe. I had been told that the wedding supper was being prepared and this banquet of love came upon me in a most wonderful trance. All of a sudden I had the revelation that as God gave me a new garment right before my natural wedding and that what I had just experienced was to tell me that my new garment was right before the wedding of the bride of Christ. The wedding of the bride was coming in the spiritual realm.

The marriage with Christ to His bride will give rise to the Miracle of the Resurrected Gentile Son. The harvest will separate the whole earth into the righteous wheat and the wicked tares. This will be the SIGN OF JONAH.

THE SIGN OF JONAH

The Sign of Jonah will be the miracle of the resurrected Gentile son (Heathen).

The sign of Jonah will be seen as the dove is brought to repentance.

The sign of Jonah will be in the fire of Tabernacles.

The sign of Jonah as the Pillar of His fire brings the earth to a great altar in the spirit.

The Sign of Jonah will be seen as Jesus come as the Lion of Judah which means, an "Altar."

The Sign of Jonah will be seen in the three battles of Armageddon and the resulting righteousness.

The Sign of Jonah will be seen in the fall of Edom.

The sign of Jonah will be seen, as He brings the humbling of the Gentiles.

The Sign of Jonah will be seen through the Chaldeans of Habakkuk and the Fall of Babylon.

The Sign of Jonah will be seen with the rise of the false prophet in the souls of God's people.

The Sign of Jonah will be seen in the separation of the nations between good and evil.

The Sign of the Great Mountain Kingdom of God, through the coming of the Manifested Son's of God.

THE TEMPLE OF THE LORD

Zechariah 1:16 *"I am returning to Jerusalem with mercy; My house shall be built in it," says the Lord of hosts, and a surveyor's line shall be stretched over Jerusalem."*

Zechariah 8:3 "I will return to Zion, and dwell in the midst of Jerusalem. Jerusalem shall be called the City of Truth, the mountain of the Lord of hosts, the Holy Mountain."

Zechariah 9:13 "And raised up your sons, O Zion, against your sons, O Greece."

The temple of the Lord will be built by the command of Cyrus, the pictured work of the Holy Spirit. Darius or Cambyses, the son of Cyrus and the fire of Christ.

Cambyses destroyed all the idols of Egypt not built for the God of heaven. Also the temple is build by the command of Artaxerxes, as King of kings and the restorer of the law into our temples. Jesus came to fulfill the law not abolish it.

The Lord will come as the Lion of the Tribe of Judah, which means, "Altar." He will bring His people into eternal righteousness. This is the Stone altar seen to break the Babylonian kingdom, as the harlot image of the world civilizations in Daniel 2:35.

The stone altar in 1 Samuel 6:14 is where they offered sacrifices of the scared cows.

When the Lord's fire brings His people out of Babylon self-rule and revives their souls, He will bring them through death to life. They will then hear the word of the Lord and do it. This Definition of Mother is in Luke 8:21. 1 Kings 17 speaks of the soul of the child of Zarephath being revived and brought to life from the upper room (The Baptism of the Holy Spirit).

This miracle of the Resurrection of the Gentile Son will be seen as the Sign of Jonah. The bride brought to repentance and filled with the Holy Spirit. Jonah means, "Dove."

The sword of the Lord will restore our soul and the restored soul will bring the body into restoration, as belief in the truth sets us free.

TEMPLE INSTRUCTIONS

John 14:6 Jesus said, *"I am the way, the Truth and the Life."*

THE WAY

The way to build our temple into Solomon's glory is laid out in the very design of the temple and the Tabernacle of Moses.

The Way is to go through the door of Christ and invite Jesus into our heart and ask him to forgive our sins and become our savior. This is a total repentance and we become born-again from heaven. Many receive Christ and that gives us the power to become the son's of God.

John 1:12 *"But as many as received Him, to them He gave the right to become children of God, to those who believe in His name: who were born not of blood, nor of the will of the flesh, nor of the will of man, but of God."*

The Way is being born-again spiritually from heaven.

Colossians 1:13 *"He has delivered us from the power of darkness and translated us into the kingdom of the Son of His love, in whom we have redemption through His blood, the forgiveness of sins."*

You receive the Holy Spirit at conversion, but we need the power in order to overcome our carnal nature and that comes only with the baptism of heaven. We not only need water baptism, but the Holy Spirit baptism

THE TRUTH

The Truth is the Holy Spirit Baptism with the spirit of truth. The Holy Spirit leads us into all truth. John 8:32 "*You shall know the truth and the truth will set us free.*"

In our walk with the Lord we walk deeper in the Temple and come into the holy place. In this place we have received the baptism of the Spirit. In the holy place is the truth.

You will receive the speaking in tongues as a prayer language, not necessarily the gift of tongues, which is used in the body of believers. How would one know that he had received the gift of power, unless there was evidence? At Pentecost in the upper room the evidence of the baptism of the Holy Spirit was the fire of tongues.

I was brought to the place of praying in tongues, which brought me to a book and deliverance.

THE LIFE IS RETURNING TO THE PRESENCE OF GOD.

When we are brought into Life and become Son's of God with the Holy Spirit we are told we will live not die. We have turned from brother Esau, as the lusts of our flesh in self-love. We have been brought into the holy of holies,

171

in which obedience to the law through the Spirit has taken place. This is spiritually the restored covenant and the reconciliation with the God of the Universe.

The holy of holies is the inner court that contains the Ark of the Covenant, also called the Ark of the Testimony.

This is the place of victory over the lies of the false prophet, also called the dragon the devil plus Satan. We defeat the devil by the blood of the Lamb and the word of our testimony.

Romans 10:10 (ten is the number of completion) *"For with the heart one believes to righteousness, and with the mouth confession is made to salvation."*

Temple instructions also include washing our clothes and to be ready for the third day. We are to purify and conquer Goliath, the great giant of who rules our flesh.

Jacob reveals that changing our garments is the putting away the foreign gods that are among us.

We are told to wash our clothes with fire and water. Water is a picture of death in some situations in the Bible. The days of Noah and the flood caused the death to the wicked. Then in the days of Elijah in the book of Kings on Mt. Carmel Elijah put water on his sacrifice and heaven came down from heaven. Water of death to sin is required to have God become a consuming fire.

The fire is seen at the top of the mountain of righteousness in Exodus 24:17 *"The sight of the glory of the Lord was like a consuming fire on the top of the mountain in the eyes of the children of Israel."*

Number 31: 23 "Everything that can endure fire, you shall put through the fire, and it shall be clean, and it shall be purified with the water of purification, but all that cannot endure fire you should put through water (die to it). Romans 7:6 "We die to the things that hold us."

We are to hide in a covenant relationship, the new covenant is the surrender of our will. Elijah was told to hide in the Brook Cherith which means, "Covenant."

We are to go through circumcision, during the fire of Tabernacles. This is the Lord separating our soul from our spirit through the beast (pride, worldly love of self brought to death) and the dragon of passion and lust and the false prophet, who brings us to the choice of which God or god of self we will worship. His lies are overcome by the word of our choice (testimony) for God over Satan.

This choice puts off our old nature and the self-rule Babylonian kingdom of the lust of the flesh, the lust of the eyes and our love of self.

We are told in Exodus 23 to hear and obey the angel of the Lord that is sent from God to bring us into the place that He has prepared for us.

TEMPLE TIMING

The temple is completed in the sixth year of Darius the Great. The reign of Darius the Great is the six years following the seven year reign of Darius the Mede also known as Cambyses.

Solomon the son of David, is a type of Christ and in historical fore-shadow Solomon's temple building takes twenty years. The word son can be defined, "Condition of."

In I Kings 6:38 it took seven years to build the houses of the Lord and in I Kings 7:1 it took 13 years to build his own house.

Solomon is a new condition of David, as a man of peace and the beloved of the Lord. The man of peace builds the Temple of the Lord. David was a man of war.

In the seven year period of Jacob's Trouble rebellion will fall, sin will fall and the desires of the world will fall from our souls.

Transfiguration into Christ and His righteousness are seen in foreshadow as the transfiguration after six days.

Matthew 17:1 *"Now after six days Jesus took Peter, James, and John his brother, brought them up on a high*

mountain by themselves, and was transfigured before them.
His face shone like the sun, and His clothes became as
white as the light."

Moses also had his face shine as he returned from the presence of God on Mount Sinai (obedience to the *law* through the Spirit) in Exodus 34:29. I am convinced that the glory that will manifest on the saints will be the glowing faces of the presence of the Lord.

"When he came down from the mountain, that Moses
did not know that the skin of his face shone while he talked
with Him." The mountain pictures righteousness.

TEMPLE JUDGMENTS

A powerful lesson was learned as my husband and three small children went to Pikes Peak to camp. We followed a large paved road that said camp grounds at the base of the mountain. We drove higher and higher and the road got narrow down to one small lane. We knew that meeting a car coming down the mountain would be an impossible situation since neither would be able to turn around. By this time we were almost perpendicular on the side of the mountain.

My husband found a tiny inlet and decided to try and turn us around. We had a camper on the back of our car and we begin to turn slowly as the gravel from the tires flew over the side of the mountain. I was praying and slowly we turned around and headed back down the mountain. Later the Lord recalled this situation to me, as He revealed that the road is wide at the bottom of His mountain of righteousness and very narrow at the top with no turning back.

"The things that you used to do you will no longer be able to do as I bring you into holiness," was a prophecy I read.

Judgments of God will involve the conditions we discussed, as to the dealing of God with Jonah to bring him to repentance.

In the fish captivity I see the fiery trial of 1 Peter 4:12. *"Beloved, do not think it strange concerning the fiery trial which is to try you, as though some strange thing happened to you."*

1 Peter 5:10 "But may the God of all grace, who called us to His eternal glory by Christ Jesus, after you have suffered a while, perfect, establish, strengthen, and settle you."

The separation of the nations will be between those that follow the Lord and those that follow the flesh. It will be during the three battles of Armageddon. We will see the fall of rebellion as the fall of Nineveh, and the fall of sin and self-will with the restored covenant and the surrender

176

of our will to the will of the Lord. The fall of the love of self Amalek happens in the Jezreel Valley. In the Jezreel Valley below Megiddo the Lord said He would break the bow of Israel in Hosea 1:5.

Megiddo is the city of the Canaanite strongholds and it lies above the Valley of Jezreel. This is the battle for our soul. Hebrews tells us to believe to the saving of our souls, which is our mind, wills and emotions.

Dagon, the Philistine god falls here before the Ark of the Covenant. Dagon is the fish god and the "Beast out of the Sea" in Revelation 13 with passion and lust as the image. "The beast out of the Earth" is then Cush, the god of confusion and Nimrod his son, the builder of Babylon self-rule kingdom. He is the false prophet that brings us to final death to self. When we choose for God over this false prophet and his lies, our Amalek self-love nature dies. *"And they loved not their lives unto the death."*

He had two horns like a lamb but spoke like a dragon. He is the "great pretender" to the Holy Spirit. Two horns depict Media-Persia and speaks to our battle between the flesh and the Spirit, that at our choice, is made whole. Our carnal nature comes under the dominion of the Holy Spirit.

Another judgment seen is the intense drought of dry heat that gets seven times hotter than normal. This drought that lies in front of the miracle of the resurrection of the Gentile son will bring the resurrection of the Gentile son as they are revived in their souls and brought back to hearing and doing the will of God.

Jude and the seducing spirits of false teachers is right before the Revelation of the living Christ and the sword of the Lord. During these false teachers we are called to contend for the faith by taking every thought captive to the obedience of Christ. Key words in Jude CONTEND FOR THE FAITH! This means stand against all temptation and take all thoughts not of God captive to the obedience of Christ.

These are sensual persons, who cause divisions, not having the spirit, flattering people to gain advantage.

I received this message in Psalm 55:21 *"The words of his mouth were smoother than butter, but war was in his heart."*

Jude mentions Enoch that prophesied these men and coming judgments of God in the latter days. Enoch was translated at the end of the seventy weeks and before the flood. He pictures the rapture for us, as God took him. Enoch had the testimony that he had pleased God before he was translated. We also need that testimony of Hebrews 11:5.

The Philadelphia church will be spared the hour of trial that comes upon the whole earth in Revelation 3:10.

While I was in Philadelphia, as a once in a lifetime experience for someone from Minnesota, I went to a church and heard the Sunday school teacher speak on the Canaanites. I had a revelation that the Philadelphia church was one that had defeated the Canaanites in their soul through the Lord and had passed from life unto death.

1 John 3:14 "We know that we have passed from death to life, because we love the brethren."

Philadelphia is the city of "Brotherly Love."

The teacher was so thrilled with the revelation that he grabbed me and swung me around the room.

TEMPLE REFINERS

Temple refiners are the horns or kings that come with the Grecian Roman beast called the eighth beast in Revelation 17 to bring us to the altar.

Psalm 118:27 *"Bind the sacrifice to the horns of the altar."*

Daniel 7:24-27 *"The ten horns are ten kings who shall arise from this kingdom. And another that shall arise after them. He shall be different from the first ones, and shall subdue three kings. He shall speak pompous words against the Most High, shall persecute the saints of the Most High*

179

and shall intend to change times and law." He subdues three kings Babylon as flesh, Egypt, as the world desires and Syria, the devil."

After 3 ½ years the kingdom shall be given to the saints of the Most High.

This beast of Revelation 17 is identified by the puzzle interpretation given us in Revelation 17. The fourth beast in Daniel is the same as the eighth beast of Revelation. Daniel started his count from Babylon where he was in time. John however, sees the entire layout of civilizations. Daniel 7:19 identifies the fourth kingdom as nails of Bronze, which was Greece and teeth of iron which was Rome. Bronze means, "fetters and chains" or what we call addictions. Iron will of power comes against the saints with the Grecian gods. Rome conquered all of Greece making the eighth one of the seven.

TEN KINGS

Ten kings come from the division of Alexander the Great's empire, following his death. His Grecian empire was divided under four generals.

Daniel 8:22 "As for the broken horn (Alexander) and the four that stood up in its place, four kingdoms shall arise out of that nation, but not with its power."

Verse 23 reveals a time span of the work of these kingdoms *"And in the latter time of their kingdom, when transgressors have reached their fullness then a king shall arise* (the false prophet of deceit that even rises against the Prince of princes) (Jesus); *but he shall be broken without human hand*" (By the fire of the Holy Spirit in the souls of God's people.)

SELEUCUS

The four generals were Seleucus that took Persia, (Iran) and Mesopotamia (Babylon (Iraq), and Syria. This reveals three kings.

LYSIMACHUS

Lysimachus took Asia Minor and Trace (Eastern Greece). Within twenty years Seleucus conquered this territory. We now have five horns or kings ruled by two generals.

CASSANDER

Cassander established Macedonia (Greece). We now have six horns under three generals.

PTOLEMY

Ptolemy took Phoenicia (Canaan) and Palestine and added it to Egypt. We now have nine kings or horns under four generals.

Daniel 8:20 tells us that Media-Persia is considered two horns. Media conquered Nineveh giving the description of our divided self as one of our enemies.

Median king was overthrown by Cyrus.

We now have ten horns or kings that were directly from the Kingdom of Alexander king of Greece.

1. Media 2 Persia is symbolic of a divided soul.

3. Babylon-Mesopotamia illustrates the flesh self-rule kingdom.

4. Syria- Assyria pictures the constant enemy of Israel as the devil.

5. Egypt and the world slavery to sin is pictured.

6. Phoenicia illustrates the Canaanite nations that oppress our soul Hosea 12:7.

7. Palestine- Philistine means "Wallowing" and sickness, self-pity, depression, loneliness, fear etc, can be seen.

8. Macedonia- Greece and worldly desires and worldly wisdom can be interpreted.

9 Asia Minor was the home of the Hittites, Assyrians, and the Scythian called Magogites, by the Greeks. Giant sins of the flesh pictured, as the Hittites are iron lusts of the flesh. Bethel was the former Hittite city of Luz, where Jacob turned from his brother Esau.

10 Trace is Eastern Greece and in it we find religious deception.

11 Another horn called the dragon, which was the devil plus Satan and he comes to the believer as the false prophet as the "Beast out of the Earth." "The beast out of the Earth" comes out of the earth in Revelation 13 and we have just had the sign of the coming false prophet, as Saddam Hussein, as the King of Babylon, crawled out from a hole in the earth.

The Lion of Judah spiritually will defeat the Lion of Babylon very soon.

TEMPLE CLEANSING

Temple cleansing will be by the Living Lord, as He promises to deliver us from the Canaanites that oppress our soul. The sword of the Lord separates our souls from our spirits by the Living Word.

Joshua 3:10 *"By this you shall know that the living God is among you and he will without fail drive out from before you the Canaanites and the Hittites and the Hivites and the Perizzites and the Girgashites and the Amorites and the Jebusites."*

Exodus 23:20-23 "Behold, I send an angel before you to keep you in the way and to bring you into the place which I have prepared. Beware of Him and obey His voice; do not provoke Him for He will not pardon your transgressions; for My name is in Him."

"But if you indeed obey His voice and do all that I speak, then I will be an enemy to your enemies and an adversary to your adversaries. For My Angel will go before you and bring you into the Amorites and the Hittites and the Perizzites and the Jebusites; and I will cut them off."

This passage goes on to say that we should not bow down before their gods and if we serve the Lord **He will take sickness away from us.**

Exodus 15:13 *"You in Your mercy have led forth the people whom You have redeemed; You have guided them in Your strength to Your holy habitation."*

Exodus 15:15-17 *"Then the chiefs of Edom will be dismayed; the mighty men of Moab, trembling will take hold of them; all the inhabitants of Canaan will melt away. Fear and dread will fall on them; by the greatness of Your arm they will be as still as a stone, till Your people pass over, O Lord, till the people pass over whom You have purchased. You will bring them in and plant them in the mountain of your inheritance, in the place, O Lord, which You have made for Your own dwelling, the sanctuary, O Lord, which Your hands have established."*

SUMMARY CONCLUSION

The Feasts of the Israelites provide us with the type of prefiguring of the stages of redemption in the New Testament believer.

The body of Christ must remove themselves from where they are camped to press on to perfection and complete redemption.

I believe that the church is going to be prepared to be led into realms of victory and glory that surpass anything we have ever known.

I am hearing in my spirit *"The glory is coming upon My people."*

The new birth is only a beginning and Pentecost or the Baptism of the Holy Spirit is not the end. God is drawing us to Himself, to holiness and to become the manifested sons of God, with the glory that is soon to be revealed.

The Feast of Trumpets in the life of the Christian is fulfilled, as we hear the call to prepare for spiritual battles and conquests. Press on to greater and greater surrender to perfect holiness and to get ready for the fullness of our personal redemption and the return of Christ to receive and establish His kingdom on earth.

The Feast of Tabernacles will be the final stage of our redemption.

This final feast as its fire offerings seen in Leviticus 23 will bring the bride to full maturity in Christ. We will pass through the veil into the presence of God and eternal life and the glory will be seen in us.

If you would like to make Christ the Lord of your life, pray this simple prayer.

Dear God,

I know that I am a sinner for all have sinned and come short of the glory of God.

I asked you to forgive my sins and cleanse me from all unrighteousness. I believe that you died to give me eternal life and I see my sins taken away by that cross. I now know that I am free of all sin and sickness, because of what Jesus Christ has done for me. I want to receive your mercy that will wash me and cleanse me of all that is not of you. I surrender my will to your will and I ask you to make me obedient to the law through the POWER of the Holy Spirit

Let me pass from death unto life with you by seeing myself crucified with Christ.

I now invite Jesus to come into my life and into my heart as my personal Savior. I am willing, by the strength of the baptism of the Holy Spirit's power to follow and obey Jesus Christ as the Lord of my life.

www.ingramcontent.com/pod-product-compliance
Lightning Source LLC
Chambersburg PA
CBHW031841090426
42741CB00005B/322

9780615153339